THAT'S WHAT I'M TALKING ABOUT

ROY FIRESTONE

FOREWORD BY BILL WALTON

Published by Magic Turtle Press

Magic Turtle Press
PO Box 56927
Sherman Oaks, CA 91413

978-0-9801122-1-4

That's what I'm talking about /
by Roy Firestone - 1st ed.

www.royfirestone.com

THAT'S WHAT I'M TALKING ABOUT

ROY FIRESTONE

Contents

Acknowledgments

This is a book that reflects my love for story telling and interviewing.

Here, I share some of my favorite moments from my more than 40 years in broadcasting.

I'd like to thank several people for helping me put it all together.

Thank you Rich Kee for the cover photo.

Thank you Susan and Ro Jaeger for your love and support.

Thanks to my boys, Andy and Nick, and my family and friends.

Thanks to editors Kim Naughton and Michael Carson.

Thanks to Jay Naughton for designing and compiling the book.

To Gary Johns, my graphic editor and my live show producer and dear friend, thank you!

I am grateful to people like Steve Edwards and Bill Walton who took the time to write an introduction and foreword to this book.

And a very special thanks to a person I have known for virtually every moment in my life.

I want to dedicate this book to my lifelong friend, David Reskin, who generously and selflessly corrected my mistakes, and put me on the proper path grammatically and creatively.

I have known David through great and hard times for both of us.

He has never asked anything of me, and gave me only loyalty, kindness and support.

He does still.

I will always be indebted to him, and his living example of courage and humanity have served to inspire me for most of my adult life.

I hope I have done him and the rest of you all proud.

Foreword
That's What I'm Talking About!

It was 30 years ago.

I had just made the most unlikely and improbable decision of my life. A decision that I had never given a single thought to; much less a second run through.

I had just chosen to become an on-air television commentator.

This was about six months after my first ankle fusion, in 1990.

I finally realized going into that surgery, my thirtieth orthopedic operation at the time, that I would never run, jump, or play basketball again ... ever.

Overwhelmed with the sadness and loss—of the life, community and purpose that was my existence for the past thirty years—I was struck by a lightning-bolt-flash of inspiration that seared across the smoking crater that is my mind.

It dawned on me right then and there, that being 6' 11", with red hair, freckles, a big nose, a goofy-nerdy looking face, being a lifelong stutterer, and a Dead-Head since I was 15, that television was really the only career possibility for me.

I couldn't get a job. Nothing. It just wasn't happening, at all.

The people who had the jobs to offer, would simply say "No."

Their explanation was always the same: "We're not putting you on TV, Walton. You'll get up there and start stuttering and spitting all over everyone and everything. Then you'll start talking about Jerry Garcia, Bob Dylan, and Neil Young; and we just can't have that."

Then one day the phone rang. It was Roy Firestone asking me to come to his ESPN *Up Close* studio in Hollywood. I'm not sure if I had ever been on Roy's now decades-long shows, *Sports Look* and *Up Close.*

I grew up in a household without a TV and I ultimately chose to be a participant, not a spectator, in the game of life.

But I did know Roy, and his shows. A little bit. Everybody in my world did.

You couldn't help but know him. He was everywhere, all the time, chasing it down and building the lives and world that we have today.

Roy gave me a chance at broadcasting. He gave me my first job at the microphone.

As we all tried to grow into better professionals, it became strikingly clear to me that Roy was very much like the great parents, teachers, and coaches that I have been blessed with throughout my life. He was genuinely interested in me, and my new teammates' success.

The whole thing became a lot of fun and something that I began to look forward to.

Roy had the skill, talent, and relaxed, natural feel of a confident leader who knew how to get the job done in a seemingly effortless way. All the while making other people better at what they do and who they are.

This was not easy to do, particularly when working with a horrendously shy stutterer who was very much afraid of everything in this new world.

But Roy and the guys stuck with me. I was blown away, and very jealous. And then we'd all be off, scattering like dust in the wind to whatever was next.

Over these last three decades I have transitioned from Roy Firestone's fan to his intern, to his project, to his student, to by far the best and most interesting part of life ... to his friend.

Now I am here to write the foreword to Roy's third book, trying to live up to the pressure and standards and emerge from beneath the massive shadows of *Up Close* (1994) and *Don't Make Me Cry, Roy* (2008).

This is a daunting challenge, because Roy, like all the people I find most interesting, is very reluctant to be the story.

He simply wants to tell it, to live it, to create it, to magnify it, and then to get on to the next one.

Roy was now the vanguard of a new sports world with his long-form, in-depth, up close look at the personalities of the burgeoning and co-mingled worlds of entertainment, sports, business, and politics.

Roy's ESPN shows became must-see-TV, his Las Vegas stage performances legendary, and his movie roles indelibly etched into our world's psyche.

Roy's intelligent, informed and conversational style became the mirror to our society. He was expertly able to transcend the game and go beyond the traditional boundaries that act as prisons for far too many of us.

With a style that incorporated the likes of Studs Terkel and Ted Koppel—with a lot of Mark Twain, Oscar Wilde and George Carlin mixed in—Roy became our moral compass, our ethical standard bearer, and the heart, spirit, and soul of our world as it could be.

Because of Roy's empathetic conscience, warm heart, and encouraging nature, he always invited his guests and friends to have their own opinions. His show became a refuge for wayward souls.

Which now brings us to Roy's newest book, *That's What I'm Talking About*.

This is a philosophical, inspirational, emotional, educational and entertaining collection of and reflection on a life well-lived, alongside a staggering cast of eclectic and electric characters, who all seem to be moving in perfect harmony as the soundtrack to Roy's melodic life—which blooms and reverberates inside our insatiable imagination and quest for more.

This is a purposefully-written compendium of Roy's fascinating, thought-provoking, and intriguing observations, opinions and essays, as he dives ever deeper into the heroes, mentors, role models, friends, and events that shaped him, and interest us.

I have grown over these last three decades to love all things Roy Firestone.

After devouring this masterpiece, which reads like a hopeful and optimistic love letter to the parade of life, I stand tall and proud, waving the flags of freedom and independence that Roy has woven for us all.

And finding at the end, that I love him more than ever.

Thank you Roy, for my life.

I will never again discount the power, value, and importance of life's lessons learned on the massage table.

That's what I'm talking about.

~ Bill Walton, 2019

Introduction

He's known for the phrase "Don't make me cry, Roy," but for me—a friend/brother for 4 decades—it's more like "Don't make me laugh, Roy."

Roy Firestone has been doing just that for all these years—making me laugh... and maybe a tear or two here and there. You see, Roy is a cocktail of sorts (even though he doesn't imbibe himself): two parts vaudevillian, one part poet, a dash of humanitarian and a tumbler of sportscaster. All mixed with a large dose of great interviewer.

But above all Roy is a storyteller. The best.

He sees the world as an ever-evolving tale of love and hate, humor and sorrow; a narrative that he finds continually fascinating and compelling, and for which, by genetics or reflex, he has the most unusual ability to share with us, to draw us in.

He loves heroes: stories of people overcoming the obstacles of living, and yet achieving. He sees the good in people but he hates the bully, and above all he reveres kindness. (however, colorful personalities get a bit of a head start in Roy's universe)

That universe has included presidents, legendary sports stars and celebrities. He's interviewed them all, always looking for the humanity, not the cheap shot. Roy wants their stories—not glib, prepared answers—because he's looking for the real answers himself.

But most of all Roy is part of that long tradition of oral history, sitting around fires in ancient times and passing on the lore of the past and the news of the present. The village crier, the minstrel. He's got a lot to say because he believes we all have a lot to say. And he wants our voices heard.

~ Steve Edwards

THAT'S WHAT I'M TALKING ABOUT

The Man With the Golden Glove

Happy Birthday to my first and really only sports hero.

Oh, I loved and admired Ali, but I never wanted to *be* like him. Brooks Robinson, who celebrated his 81st birthday recently, carried himself with grace, dignity, and class. I wanted to be like him, even though I would never have his talent. I wanted to carry myself with dignity and decorum. I hoped that if ever I were successful, I would embody the qualities I saw in Brooks.

From the time I was five years old I knew he was the player who would be at the center of my sports universe. By the time I was 18, and he was almost retired, I saw him "Up Close."

For two years in the late 60's I was batboy for the Baltimore Orioles during spring training.

In truth, for me the job was a gateway to Brooks Robinson. I thought I might get to meet him, get to know him, and maybe, just maybe, become, dare I say, a "friend" of Brooks?

On my very first day as an Oriole batboy, Brooks Robinson—always the first player in both the clubhouse and locker room (sometimes ahead of the clubhouse "cubbies")—walked into my tiny dressing room.

"Hey partner," he said. "What's your name?"

I looked up from what I was doing and saw Brooks with his hand extended to me. It took my breath away. After I stammered and remembered my name, he said, "Partner, wanna play some pepper?"

For those who don't know: "Pepper" is a simple game of hit and field. For the next 30 minutes, a goofy, awkward kid from Miami is playing ball with his only sports hero. "Don't stab at it, partner," he said. "Look the ball in."

Brooks Robinson was giving me fielding pointers. I eventually caught my breath, and for the next several months I would ride "shotgun" on the buses going to away games in the spring with Brooks Robinson.

We talked, but he was so friendly and interested in me, I could barely say anything at all. He just radiated positivity and goodness. Brooks never dissed. No gossip. No profanity. He was always the gentleman of the team, and the team had a lot of profane, bad mannered types. Brooks lived the authentic perception people have of him. He exuded the best of sportsmanship, cheerfulness, and positivity. I must have watched him field 10,000 ground balls.

He never took time to goof off when he was "working." Years passed. I left the team to go to college. One night, the Orioles were playing my college team, Miami, in a spring exhibition game. I was the play-by-play announcer on college radio with my buddy Gary Chrisman (who is, to this day, one of the best in the business). Brooks Robinson comes to the plate and hits a home run ... and Gary and I were calling the game.

I can say I called a Brooks Robinson home run on a radio broadcast.

More years went by. Brooks went to the Hall of Fame. We remained close. Brooks developed some serious health issues but thankfully he recovered. One night, when he was ill, he asked me to fill in for him at a major awards banquet. I couldn't have said yes fast enough. It was an undeserved honor for me.

Let's fast forward to 2012. I get a phone call and my caller ID says, "Brooks Robinson."

"Partner, it's Brooks Robinson," he says (like I don't know who Brooks is). "They are unveiling my statue at Oriole Park at Camden Yards, and I'd like you to introduce me to the fans when I come to the podium."

I literally looked at the phone the way people do in movies: with disbelief. He wanted me, of all people, to dedicate his statue with him? It made no sense. Then I realized. He didn't want to pick one teammate or baseball person he was close with. And here's why.

Brooks cares about people's feelings. If he'd asked Earl Weaver or Frank Robinson to introduce him, maybe someone else who played with him might be hurt. That's the way Brooks thinks. It is why he is a great and good man. He picked me. What an honor.

The day comes. Thousands of people are there for Brooks' statue. I am introduced by Gary Thorne at Oriole Park. I walk to the podium. I'm choked up. I almost can't breathe. But this isn't about me. It's about my only sports hero. This is the greatest honor of my public life. After I catch my breath, I get a few minutes to tell my hero that I love him. I get to tell everyone there why.

We could sure use a ton of people like you on this planet, Brooks. I love you, Brooks Robinson. You're the greatest man in sports I ever knew.

Head and Shoulders Above the Rest

The first time I met Wilt he was driving a $250,000 Rolls Royce convertible. He had a giant spotted Great Dane in the back seat and a gorgeous blonde "friend" in the passenger seat. He wore a silver and purple silk jumpsuit, a burgundy beret, neon colored scarves, tangerine-tinted sunglasses and no shoes. At the time he was 7 feet 2 inches tall and weighed about 320 pounds. I asked him if he would like to come on my show. Wilt said, "I'd love to come on, Roy, but I'm trying to keep a low profile."

It could've been the funniest comeback line I've ever heard from any athlete or celebrity, but Wilt was actually serious. The problem was, Wilt couldn't *ever* "keep a low profile," not with that body, that mystique, that incandescent persona, and the enormous, almost folk-hero reputation he brought to almost everything he did.

The 20,000 women he, *ahem*, knew, was a ridiculous estimate,

likely invented to sell his book. But he never did marry. In the time I knew him I don't think he ever had a serious relationship with a woman.

He loved to play beach volleyball (mostly against women), but was a serious fan of all women's sports and attended many women's sporting events in Los Angeles.

He loved to drive across the country and kept personal records of how quickly he did it. I think he once drove from California to Philadelphia in 2 days.

Wilt scored 100 points in a single game on March 2, 1962 in Hershey, Pennsylvania. Every year, on the anniversary of that game, I marvel that this feat may never be broken in a regulation NBA game.

Wilt was just 63 years old when he died in his sleep from cardiac arrest. I couldn't believe it when I heard. I thought this was the one man who would live forever. But it turns out Wilt had had heart trouble for years, and feared dying young.

I absolutely loved this guy. Not every member of the press would say that. He could be rude, standoffish, and intimidating. But for some reason Wilt got a kick out of me, and he allowed a somewhat jovial, deeply personal, sometimes touching, and even haunting 15 minutes in the studio. I know I'll never meet another man in sports like Wilt. It wasn't just the size of the body. It was the size of the spirit that made him truly "head and shoulders above the rest."

A Session in Class

Let's talk about something we don't see much of anymore. Class. I consider "class" a verb, not a noun because class takes action, but never in a showy way.

Many people think class has something to do with money. It does not. Class is earned but having class has little to do with, well, "class." That is, there are affluent people who have class, but blue collar people and people in poverty who have it as well. I've seen some of the wealthiest, most powerful people present themselves in a totally classless way.

Class never has been about wealth or power and never will be.

Class is quiet, dignified action.

People with class never ever talk about themselves. They live it. Unfortunately we don't see true class much anymore because many have become obsessed with self-promotion, loud talk, hype, and attention. Our society pays attention to and rewards those people first. But class is deliberately muted by people who have it.

When I think of class, I think of my world of sports.

I think of Arnold Palmer. Brooks Robinson. Al Kaline. Steve Young. Merlin Olsen. David Robinson. Tim Tebow.

Class was Art Rooney. Roger Staubach. Willie Stargell.

Paul Warfield had class. Paul Warfield scored 85 touchdowns in his career and never danced in the end zone, never spiked the football. He handed the ball quietly to the referee. He knew what he had done. He didn't have to remind you of himself. He's in the Hall of Fame for his accomplishments, but he would easily get into the Hall of Fame of Class.

Arthur Ashe had class. Roberto Clemente. John Wooden, too.

I've met scores of women with class. Althea Gibson. Peggy Fleming.

I always felt Martina Navratilova had class and people got that about her.

Class was Wilma Rudolph, and Billie Jean King.

Class was Katarina Witt and Donna De Varona.

Tom Landry. Derek Jeter, Tony Gwynn, Cal Ripken, Jr., and Albert Pujols all have it. Sandy Koufax lived a life of class and so did Vin Scully and Jack Buck.

Stan Musial—he was indeed, "The Man."

Class is grace, and class is sometimes manifested in gestures, but it is a quality above all that isn't about one thing or another. Class is lived and shown in subtle ways. Class is about honor, character, and commitment to doing the right thing, the good thing, the wise thing.

Bart Starr had class.

Chris Evert, even for her mistakes in marriage, always exuded class to me. *And that's the thing.* Having class doesn't mean a person doesn't have flaws or doesn't make mistakes in life.

I think Kareem Abdul-Jabbar always had class.

Tony Romo had it. Emmitt Smith too.

Gale Sayers was one of the classiest people I ever met. Gail Devers also.

Class is a commitment to offering humanity something of ourselves ... but never in a prideful, loud way.

Class never ever seeks attention. Class is deeply influential, too. People who spend time around those with class often become a person with class themselves. Class is living life with honor, quiet strength, and patience.

Jim Mckay had class. Bob Costas, too.

Hank Aaron. Clayton Kershaw. Jack Nicklaus.

Class is deep self-confidence without cockiness. It is the quality of self-awareness and sure-footedness.

Ann Landers once said it best: "Class never runs scared."

I've left a ton of people off this list I'm sure, but this wasn't supposed to be a complete inventory anyway. I just wanted to say class these days isn't in abundance, but it certainly can be found if you look. Try and spend your time around people with class. These are people with inner peace, integrity, manners, humility, and grace.

We could sure use a lot more of those people in this world.

A Pain in
My Pinstripes

This is a true story. You can ask Tino Martinez. He was there.

I could never and would never root for the Yankees, even if they gave me a million dollars. George Steinbrenner once brought me in to speak at a Yankee banquet for the U.S. Olympic Foundation in Tampa, Florida. It was a charity event and it was all in good fun. It was almost a "roast" of George. He liked my impressions and musical bits. The show went well. At the end of the dinner, George came on stage and brought me a Yankee jersey and a Yankee hat and wanted me to pose for a picture wearing it. He knew I was a former batboy for the Orioles and a ridiculous over-the-top Orioles fan. He started needling me about the Orioles being lousy and to "come on over" and be a Yankee fan. I refused to put the hat on and I certainly wouldn't wear the jersey. Steinbrenner started laughing and said, "What would you say about our Yankees?" I said (as loud as I could), "Yankees suck!" Steinbrenner, thank God, laughed loud and hard and I was able to get off the stage without wearing his gear.

I always got along well with George. He had many likable qualities to go with his dark side. But if he were alive, I'd tell him again, "Yankees suck!" (Actually they don't suck on the field, but as a concept? Yep, they suck.)

A Wonderful Woman

In an increasingly harsh, cruel, and difficult world, with more and more cynicism and division every day, I believe it inspires and uplifts us to tell a story of a simple act of kindness and love.

You know Gal Gadot, who almost out of nowhere became a superstar for her portrayal of Wonder Woman. Before that, she had a role in the action movie series *Fast and Furious*.

She's not just a beauty. She has a fascinating backstory. Her family survived the Holocaust and emigrated to Israel after the war. As a young woman Gal served in the Israeli military, where she was a combat instructor.

A few weeks ago, while filming the sequel to her *Wonder Woman* smash hit in Washington, D.C., Gal learned of a family in Falls Church, Virginia whose child was dealing with leukemia and waiting for a bone marrow transplant. Gal told her agent that she wanted to go to the hospital to spread some cheer and lift some spirits, but she wanted to go in full costume, as "Wonder Woman."

There are scores of stories of celebrities and athletes going to hospitals, but it's rare for a person to go in full costume openly and willingly because they know that's what young people would expect of them.

Kelly Swink Sahady thanked the actress for spending time with her daughter Karalyne. "We're fans for life now," Sahady said in her GoFundMe Page video.

Gal's name in Hebrew means "wave," and she brought a wave of joy to Inova Hospital.

Maybe we could all use a wave of goodness in this world.

I thought of Eleanor Roosevelt, another kind of "Wonder Woman" in her time, almost forgotten these days.

She said this once:

"If human beings can be trained for cruelty and greed and a belief in power which comes through hate and fear and force, certainly we can train equally well for greatness and mercy and the power of love which comes because of the strength of the good qualities to be found in the soul of every human being."

Gal Gadot never met Eleanor Roosevelt, may have never even heard of her, but the "wonder" of both women is in their sense of love and goodness. You don't have to have super powers to help lift the world. You just need to take whatever goodness you have and spread it anywhere someone needs it.

That's the superpower that the world needs more than ever—*love*.

A Comet's Promise

I've had so many joys and honors in my life, but the truth is that as a kid I dreamed of one day performing in a Las Vegas showroom. It's kind of in my DNA. I was a child performer in little clubs on Miami Beach before I was 13. I wasn't great, but I loved to do impressions. That was authentically me.

Knowing me for decades only as a sportscaster and journalist, some might have been put off by the fact that - yes, I'll admit it - I led dual life (as broadcaster and performer). Because isn't a TV interviewer supposed to stay in his lane and not entertain audiences in showrooms? You can't be both, they might have said. Well, they can feel whatever they want, but there's no way I couldn't be a performer.

One night the Golden Nugget's then-CEO, Steve Wynn, caught my act at the Riviera Country Club. He was stunned. He didn't know I sang or did impressions and comedy, and asked if I'd be interested in playing the Nugget with Lou Rawls. I whipped out a pen: Where do I sign? Lou Rawls has always been one of my all-time favorite singers, and his son is a FB friend.

To tell you the truth it could've been Lou Grant and I'd have been thrilled to fulfill my dream of playing Vegas. What I couldn't have known at the time was that opening night would bring another kind of thrill: seeing someone I admired and loved from the sports world in the audience.

Fast forward about a month or so later. The legendary Gale Sayers was on my show. "The Kansas Comet", as he'd been known in college, had seen me perform at fundraisers and asked if I was "ever gonna do Vegas". He was half kidding. I looked him in the eye and said, "As a matter of fact I'll be there this coming Dec. 8th... which also happens to be my birthday!"

Gale told me, "Roy, I'll fly in for opening night." That was nice I thought, even just to make me feel good. I knew he didn't mean it.

On my birthday I co-headlined with Lou Rawls (one of my true musical idols). Shortly before the curtain there was a knock on my dressing room door: it was Gale Sayers. To say that I was stunned is an understatement. I would have cried, but I had a show to do in 5 minutes. Gale actually adjusted my tie and gave me a pep talk. "Roy, you don't need to be pumped up. You can do this. I've seen it. I'll be in the front row cheering you on."

Yes. Gale Sayers was giving me the "Everything's coming up roses 'Ethel Merman effect!'" (You'll be swell... you'll be great, and so forth.)

Then Lou sauntered in. We all chatted and took pictures... and I was on another planet with excitement. They announce me, I go on for maybe 30 minutes and get TWO standing ovations: both led by Gale Sayers.

Lou Rawls then took the stage and insisted I come back out. He asked the audience to tell me how great my debut was. The response was truly emotional for me and deeply appreciated. It was absolutely one of the greatest thrills in my career, and fulfilled that dream I'd had since I was nine years old.

As you may know, Gale Sayers has had some serious health issues lately. Thousands of fans who love him, like me, have him in their hearts always. I'm told Gale struggles with dementia likely caused by CTE. As I write this he's in a wheelchair and unfortunately doesn't remember many names or faces.

He surely wouldn't remember me. But I'll never forget him, not just for his greatness as an athlete but for his incredibly kind gesture at my debut performance in Las Vegas.

We all stand for Gale. He's one of the finest people I've known anywhere in life -- let alone the most exciting running back I've ever seen. I love Gale Sayers. This man kept his promise to me.

And I promise that I'll always keep him in my heart. I hope you will too.

The Hits Keep Coming

Superstar record producer David Foster has earned 16 Grammys and has been a music producer for some of the greatest names in musical history, including Chaka Khan, Alice Cooper, Christina Aguilera, Andrea Bocelli, Toni Braxton, Michael Bublé, Chicago, Natalie Cole, Celine Dion, Kenny G, Josh Groban, Whitney Houston, Jennifer Lopez, Kenny Rogers, Seal, Rod Stewart, Charice, Donna Summer, Olivia Newton-John, Madonna, Mary J. Blige, Michael Jackson, Cheryl Lynn, and Barbra Streisand.

But David once told me how his biggest hit nearly killed someone.

On the night of June 9, 1992, David was driving his SUV on the Pacific Coast Highway when a man ran out of the darkness and into his path. David couldn't avoid him. His car hit the man and sent him flying.

When paramedics arrived they found that the victim had suffered head trauma and a broken left leg. They also noticed a hematoma. They instantly relieved pressure on his brain and stabilized him.

Doctors later determined that the hematoma could not have been a result of the accident. In fact it had been caused by an earlier trauma, and without proper medical attention would have killed him.

That man was entertainer Ben Vereen!

After four hours of surgery, Vereen woke up: and David was there. They told Vereen what had happened. He realized that his life was actually saved because of David's accident and proper medical attention! Vereen looked at David (whom he knew well) and said, "David, for all the hits you've made, this one was the best ... Good hit, David!"

They call David Foster the "hitmaker." Now the hitmaker can call himself the "hitmaker-lifesaver."

The Fan-in-Chief

First, to say I had differences with the man would be a massive understatement. My family and I despised his policies, and he had said things that were deeply anti-Semitic, but I won't mention any of that stuff here.

Back in 1993 we got a call from the Nixon Library requesting me to interview the 37th President of the United States. He wanted to talk baseball only. That was the only ground rule.

When I arrived at his library in California I was a bit nervous, one of the very few times I was ever nervous doing a TV interview (and I've been fortunate enough to do 5,000 interviews). And I was taken aback—and a little intimidated—by Nixon's friendliness. He

wasn't physically tall or imposing, but here was Richard Nixon. He had done very, very few interviews post-Watergate.

We started the interview and Nixon was eager, opinionated, and super knowledgeable.

It wasn't like talking to Bill James, but Nixon knew his stuff. We talked about the dead-ball era and 1930s baseball. He loved players like Ruth and Gehrig, but he knew a great deal about players like Hack Wilson, and, of course, he knew Ted Williams.

The interview was fascinating and fun, and Nixon was really enjoying it. When we had to stop to change tapes for the camera, he leaned over to me and said:

"Hey, Roy, ya know what show I really like of yours? The show with your dad. Give him my best."

This stunned me. My pop hated Nixon and his policies, but this was so astonishing to me that A) he'd even watched my show and B) he loved the one with my dad.

Anyway, Nixon was light, loose, and happy. We playfully argued about who was better at many baseball positions. I loved Brooks Robinson of course, easily my favorite player of all time. Nixon was prepared for that, because he already knew this about me. "Brooks was a great defensive player," Nixon said, "but Mike Schmidt could hit with power and field too, and so could Eddie Mathews." I told Nixon that I respected that opinion but Brooks was always in my heart.

We finished the 2-hour shoot. As we were packing up Nixon actually looked a bit sad. He pulled me aside and said, "C'mon, Roy, let's go have a drink and talk more baseball." I couldn't believe it.

Neither of us were real drinkers (I've never even had as much as a beer in my life), but Nixon wasn't looking for the booze. He was looking for a baseball friendship.

I had to turn him down because I needed a ride home from my crew.

I realized Nixon was very, very lonely. Baseball was his safe haven for conversation.

It actually hurt me to turn him down (the Secret Service wasn't very keen on me hanging around either).

Anyway, the interview ends and I run to a pay phone to call

my father. I get him on the phone and start to tell him about the interview.

Me: "Dad, I just interviewed Richard Nixon."

Dad: "That man was a criminal, and a crook. I hated the SOB."

Me: 'Wait, pop. He just said he saw the show you did with me on Father's Day. It's his *favorite show of all time*!"

Long pause from my father, and then this: "Well, you know, Nixon did many *great* things. He was a very accomplished President. Russia. China ...."

This cracked me up. If Vladimir Putin had given my father a compliment, he'd had been friends with him.

As I look back at that interview, one thing remains clear: Baseball, more than any sport, provides people who are wildly different in ideology, style, temperament, and political opinions a safe haven to talk, laugh, argue in good fun—to just enjoy each other's company.

I truly enjoyed meeting and spending time with Richard Nixon. Baseball was a unifier. A language. And yes, for two hours, Nixon and I were pals. Unbelievable. That's why, to me, baseball is the greatest game in the world. It's a gift that keeps on giving.

Love, Faith and Healing

I used to work as a contributor on the Los Angeles morning news show *Good Day LA*.

The mood on the set was light, chatty, and informative. Like all such programs it had to carry sunniness, cheerfulness, and an upbeat tone. After all, people were rising and getting ready for work. The mantra was buoyancy and exuberance, all the better to help people get their motors revving.

I loved the people I worked with. Most of the anchors were quick-witted and positive. There was one woman who always caught my eye—not merely because she was beautiful and talented but also because she exuded a spunky, playful, human warmth that was contagious in the best of ways. Her name is Maria Quiban, and if you live in Los Angeles and watch *GDLA* she is hard to miss. These morning shows are highly competitive. Every day Maria broadcasts the weather and other segments in the second largest media market in the country.

One day she popped into the green room to say hello. She was excited because she and her husband Sean would be celebrating Sean's 50th birthday with a dream trip to Paris. They had never been to Paris. I was happy for both of them and shared some restaurant and tourist type recommendations.

But something happened on that dream vacation that would change Maria's life forever. Once in Paris, Sean, normally energetic and athletic, began to feel tired all the time.

He was continually lying down. He seemed disoriented and would lose things, which was not like him at all. Then Maria remembered that earlier in the year the very organized Sean brought home someone else's car keys. Not only hadn't he realized that they weren't his, he couldn't even remember how he acquired them in the first place. That was one of a few other instances when he didn't seem himself.

They decided that when they got back home they would have him checked out. Bloodwork and a basic medical exam revealed nothing out of the ordinary. But Sean seemed in a constant state of fatigue, and his forgetfulness and disorientation worried Maria. Unconvinced by the initial diagnosis, they saw more doctors—including a neurologist who ordered a scan. At his recommendation they ended up at the Brain Surgery Center at St. John's Hospital in Santa Monica.

It was there that doctors showed them the lesions on Sean's brain for the first time. A biopsy confirmed their worst fears: Sean had *glioblastoma multiforme* (GBM), the most aggressive form of brain cancer and the killer of people like Senator Ted Kennedy, Beau Biden (son of Vice-President Joe Biden), and Senator John McCain.

About 25,000 patients a year are diagnosed with this rare cancer. The survival rate for most is two years or less.

Maria and Sean were devastated.

"I remember walking out of that exam room and Sean pulling away from my grip to sink into a quiet corner to weep. 'I'm so sorry,' he said."

Maria at first believed her husband would recover. She held onto false hope because another anchorwoman on the show had survived an operable brain tumor. But Sean's tumors were different. He had inoperable GBM, the deadliest form and a disease that receives little research funding.

At first Sean was healthy enough to do things with his family. Maria, Sean, and their young son Gus made sure they lived life with fun and joy, and recorded many moments on video. Aware that dark clouds were on the horizon they went to Disneyland, New York and Hawaii—Maria's adopted home in her youth. She said,

If there's the slightest positive in this horrible disease it's that you do take every single day as a gift. We treated each day as if it were a month. A month becomes a year when you are on borrowed time. Every day is another opportunity to love your family and cherish everything you have more than you ever would otherwise.

As expected, Sean's condition worsened and Maria had to take a medical leave from the show. She devoted all of her time to Sean and Gus. After educating herself she became a kind of nurse for Sean, changing IV fluids and other important tasks.

Our love became a deeper kind of love, the kind I had never experienced. We talked openly about it. We shared many tears but also many laughs. Yes, I had terrifying moments, but I knew I had to be strong and focused and tend to my family. We had tremendous support. Sean has five brothers and sisters-in-law, and his parents and my parents were there for us too, along with the rest of our family members and friends. We had help around the clock. I loved my extended family even more.

Sean Whitesell died on December 28, 2015. He was 52 years old.

I hear people say things like, 'One day at a time.' 'Give yourself time to grieve,' and I did that. But I needed to work, first because

cancer is expensive and I needed that job. But also because I needed to come back to the people I loved and the work I enjoyed. Yes, it was exhausting, but it was a much different kind of exhaustion than I felt at home.

Going back to work after Sean died helped me cope with the pain and loss. Putting a smile on my face for the public... some days it was more forced. But once you have that smile on, well, it's just easier to keep it on. It became a kind of costume, but in a good way, and ultimately in an authentic way.

Maria continued.

When I was 7 years old my father drowned. I watched my family fall apart. But my mother was very strong, and I looked to her as my son Gus looks to me now...a human safety net.

She paused and said, "My mother never failed us, and I will do my best to never fail my son."

Maria continued.

Every single day. I get in my car, and while some people think I'm talking on a speakerphone at a red light, I am speaking directly to Sean. When I have a tough day with Gus, I'll say to Sean. 'Can you please help me? Can you take care of this?' I wear his wedding band every single day. I remember he got so thin it fell off his hand. So I put it on...and I've never taken it off.

Maria is a devout Catholic who attends mass every week

People ask me if I'm angry at God. To tell the truth, there were many times that I was. But I have learned to replace anger with gratitude. I'm grateful for my life, and my family's life and my son's life.

Trauma causes you to build walls around your heart. I have to remember I'm in charge of another little human being, and so I focus on him first. I have confidence and trust in God, and Sean, still, and in the universe. I've had a kind of love that some people will probably never experience and for that I will always be grateful.

Less than two months after losing Sean, Maria went to church on a Sunday, and again, she spoke to Sean.

I was in real pain, and I asked Sean to do something, anything, to show me he was with me. Suddenly there was a commotion at the back: former Vice President Joe Biden was visiting. I remembered that his son Beau had lost his battle with GBM only a few weeks earlier. We had this shared trauma, shared loss. And I truly believe Sean made this happen. I waited until the service was over and asked the secret service officers if I could have a word. They motioned him over. He smiled and said hello and at first was interested in Gus—asking him how he was.

Then Maria said this:

"Mr. Biden, I share your grief and your loss. My husband Sean died from GBM only a few weeks ago."

Suddenly Biden's focus changed. His smile stopped and he looked up at me and said this:

Listen to me. You will, one day, maybe not next year, maybe not two years from now, but ONE day, you will say Sean's name and you will smile instead of cry. You take care of your little boy. I promise you will be happy again.

I was in my car not long after my interview with Maria and a song came on the radio. The song was "Tears in Heaven," written by Eric Clapton after he lost his 4 year-old son Conor in a tragic accident. The lyrics were shared with Will Jennings, who also wrote "Up Where We Belong." As I listened I couldn't stop thinking of Maria and her grief. The lyrics read:

Time can bring you down
Time can bend your knees
Time can break your heart
Have you begging please, begging please.
Beyond the door
There's peace I'm sure
And I know there'll be no more
Tears in heaven.

I told Maria about this and she paused for a long while before responding.

It's true. I believe that Sean will be in heaven with me in the next life. I know I will see him again. I know I will feel him again. But now I must build my trust in God and in living, loving, and learning.

My last question had to do with the power of devotion—to her child, her work, her faith, her life. She said this:

"Devotion is a human investment in life. But that return of devotion is the greatest reward of all."

Maria Quiban remains a person of devotion. She's writing her own book, *Still Smiling* (DaCapo Publishing), about her ordeal with GBM. She has spoken on behalf of Global Genes and Rare Disease Advocates. Last month in Washington D.C she connected with policy makers about a new Global Genes-funded study that highlights the negative effects (physical and emotional) on caregivers while caring for loved ones with rare and terminal diseases. She was there to share her unique experience in the hope of changing some of our current policies to reflect more support for caregivers.

And so Maria Quiban, the cheerful morning anchor, carries on. Some days are better than others. Some days are just plain hard. But she's devoted to her son, and her work, and her family. She says every day is for "living, loving, and learning."

Baseball in a Different World

A few years ago I was given an assignment to cover professional baseball in Japan. Things have changed since of course, but there were some profound differences between the American game and the way the Japanese play.

First, let's discuss the preparation.

Spring training was like training at Parris Island. It was a boot camp—constant running, sprinting, drills and more drills during the day, and even more drills at night. I was exhausted just watching it.

Japanese baseball is physically demanding every day, even on "off days," because there aren't really "off days." Five hours before the game started in Tokyo, I saw pitchers running stadium steps for 30 minutes. Even the ones pitching that night! I saw the entire team run through vigorous calisthenics, sit-ups, pushups, jumping jacks, and running in place. Batting practice and fielding drills could last an hour or more. Players worked on bunting drills for maybe another hour. Japanese teams had video classes as an entire team, with scouting reports and firsthand accounts.

Some of these meetings would last a couple of hours.

The Japanese ballplayer, with some exceptions, was limited in power, but extremely well-coached and fundamentally sound. No matter your position on the team, if you couldn't bunt, you weren't there for long. The Japanese baseball player is all about team first and individual accomplishments second. Sacrifice is, both metaphorically and literally, the key to success.

At the time I was there no facial hair was allowed—no beards, no mustaches, no sideburns. Plus, almost all the players had short hair because long hair was frowned upon.

Then there were the fans. I couldn't believe what I saw. They came to watch batting practice at 4 p.m., straight from work, arriving on a bullet train. The fans arrived as a company. It was the Mitsubishi section over here, the Toyota section over there, Sanyo over there. They would bring noisemakers, drums, confetti, horns, and they would generate a non-stop din throughout the game. Every inning of every game seemed like it was bases loaded, two outs, and a 3-2 pitch. When players made even routine plays, an enormous roar erupted from the crowd.

The level of respect between umpire and players was unreal. I saw one umpire take a field mic, bow and literally apologize to the whole stadium for a wrong call! I saw a player bow to a pitcher after the pitcher had struck him out. Arguing or confronting an opponent or umpire was a major scandal. If you even touched an opponent or umpire in a dispute, it was considered grounds for a permanent ban from the game. Even the scoreboard was something to see. Instead of "Go Giants" on the video screen, you'd see elaborate color graphics with literate and detailed cheers like (translation):

We shall persevere against our formidable opponents,
the "Carp," for whom we have great respect.

And then I saw something else on the scoreboard.

Numbers kept flashing.

"45, 38, 41, 40, 39, 40."

I was mesmerized. What could it mean? I asked my interpreter.

It wasn't the number of pitches, or the pitch speed, it was the "wind impact" on every pitch. The Japanese *love* data. On the scoreboard they included grass/turf numbers for players. Night and day. February vs. March. OPS. OBP. UZR. All of it. It covered the entire scoreboard!

The newspaper coverage was also unreal. They would run 8 or 9 pages of color photos with pages of interviews, all for a Wednesday game in the middle of the season. A routine game was like the World Series.

I could go on and on, but there was one moment I watched on TV that blew my mind.

The manager came on a morning talk show in *full uniform* ... and it was in the off-season! They showed a highlight of the MVP of the Japanese Championship Series winning a car for his accomplishments. But unlike in the old days here in the States, they didn't deliver the car at his home stadium until a month or so later. They drove it onto the field, the MVP got in, and then he drove out of the stadium waving to the fans the whole way!

Yeah, baseball is baseball, I guess. But baseball in Japan is in a different world.

90 Degrees in the Snow

I watch *It's a Wonderful Life* every year on Christmas Eve. The story moves me every time, and inspires me with its message of kindness, charity, compassion, and human decency in the face of greed, avarice, and contempt for the poor and working class. It seems even more relevant now than ever before.

It's an amazing film and script for a lot of reasons. First, the movie was filmed about two blocks from my house in Encino, California in the dog days of a hot summer in 1946. All those winter scenes were shot in more than 90-degree heat on the RKO sets outdoors. Running through the "snow" all bundled up in layers of heavy clothing, Jimmy Stewart nearly suffered from heat stroke. Also, the film—which lost over a half million dollars when it was released—was nominated for five Academy Awards and won exactly none.

The classic film is based on a short story by Philip Van Doren Stern. A writer and historian, Stern was moved to write it after having a dream about Charles Dickens' *A Christmas Carol*. He called the story "The Greatest Gift," and the plot follows a very similar path to that of *It's a Wonderful Life*. It took him four years to write 4,000 words, and when he finally finished it in 1943, he struggled to find a publisher. Instead, that December Stern printed 200 copies himself and sent them to friends as a Christmas card. One fell into the hands of film producer David Hempstead, who showed it to Cary Grant. Grant fancied himself in the lead role, and Hempstead's production company bought the film rights in April, 1944. Frank Capra then acquired those rights for $10,000 and cast James Stewart as George Bailey.

Donna Reed was just 25 years old when she portrayed Mary, and James Stewart was 38. The chemistry between them was remarkable. The famous scene in which Mary and George are sharing a phone takes your breath away. The smoldering attraction between them is powerful, moving, and sensual… and all of it without a single inference to sex.

One of the people who found *It's a Wonderful Life* easy to resist was Karolyn Grimes, otherwise known as ZuZu, the ringleted youngest daughter in the Bailey Family. In fact she hadn't even seen it until 1979—34 years after she delivered that final heartstring-pulling line *"Every time a bell rings an angel gets his wings"*—but has now watched it over 500 times.

Grimes didn't exactly have the time to enjoy the film-release merriment: she was orphaned at 15 and sent to live with her strictly religious aunt and uncle by court order. She married, divorced, and raised two children single-handedly after her second husband died in a hunting accident. Her third husband (who had three children of his own as well as a further two with Grimes) died of cancer shortly after her teenage son committed suicide.

The film was not only a flop in 1946, it was identified by Ayn Rand as one of the more pernicious threats to Americanism, and was subject to an investigation for communist beliefs by the FBI and the House Un-American Activities Committee (HUAC). They found that George Bailey's story contained several subversive tendencies, including "demonizing bankers," "attempts to instigate class warfare," and was "written by communist sympathizers."

It's a Wonderful Life isn't a light Christmas comedy—in fact for much of the film it's a deeply dark drama—but I believe *Life* is my favorite all-time film, and every year it brings me renewed hope, optimism and good feelings for the future of humanity.

The Boss of Broadway

If you'd gone to *Springsteen on Broadway* looking for a high energy, balls out, hold-no-prisoners, rock-my-soul night from the greatest rocker of them all, you went to the wrong place. This show was not that, not at all.

This was Bruce in words and not in kinetic energy. But for me it wasn't disappointing on any level. To the contrary, it was revelatory. Because this was Bruce baring his soul, telling his story, with mostly just his guitar, and occasionally his piano.

He was funny and self-effacing, tender and sentimental, and *literary*. To me it was like listening to John Steinbeck with a guitar. Bruce, reciting passages from his best selling book, told his real story. He wasn't a blue collar, punch-the-clock factory worker or auto

mechanic as he is sometimes represented in his songs. In fact, Bruce said he'd never worked 5 days in any one week in any one job in his life until this stint on Broadway. "I am a fraud," he joked.

He didn't burnish his image. He mocked it.

He then moved me with powerful stories of his family growing up in Long Branch, New Jersey and later in Asbury Park, where he was waiting to "be discovered" with his kick-ass bar band. It never happened. "Nobody is coming to Asbury Park," he said. He spoke powerfully of the broken shell of a man that was his father. His father carried a dozen jobs, all briefly. He was an alcoholic and battled depression, and a young Bruce saw this shattered life and literally had to pull his father out of a bar nightly. He spoke movingly of his mother, a tender, upbeat, cheerful woman who knew how to love, and did it well.

Throughout this show Springsteen offered recollections of his rise and ambition, of cross-country car trips to get to a single gig in California. Back then he didn't even know how to drive. But he had to get to the gig. So he just took the wheel, stayed on a straight line and navigated across America with help from his buddy in the passenger seat. They made the gig.

This show is about Bruce Springsteen's life when he wasn't "The Boss" but just a teenager with a dream to escape the life his father knew. For the rest of his life, consciously or unconsciously, Bruce played thousands of gigs with the idea that somehow he could make his father's pain go away when he saw his son succeed at something.

The show was a two-hour soliloquy about everything from the longing to make something of a life earmarked for despair and dead-ended disappointment to hope and promises made. He spoke and sang movingly and powerfully about Clarence Clemens, his saxophone player who died six years ago—"The Big Man." Bruce said this:

Standing together we were badasses, on any given night, on our turf, some of the baddest asses on the planet. We were united, we were strong, we were righteous, we were unmovable, we were funny, we were corny as hell and as serious as death itself. And we were coming to your town to shake you and to wake you up. Together, we told an older, richer story about the possibilities of friendship that transcended those I'd written in my songs and in my music. Clarence carried it in his heart. It was a story where the Scooter and the Big Man not only busted the city in half, but we kicked ass and remade the city, shaping it into the kind of place where our friendship would not be such an anomaly. And that, that's what I'm gonna miss. The chance to renew that vow and double down on that story on a nightly basis, because that is something, that is the thing that we did together, the two of us. Clarence was big, and he made me feel, and think, and love, and dream big. How big was the Big Man? Too fucking big to die. And that's just the facts. You can put it on his gravestone. You can tattoo it over your heart. Accept it. It's the New World. Clarence doesn't leave the E Street Band when he dies. He leaves when we die.

It was passages like that one that hit me in my soul. I began weeping, and people in my row were also weeping. That evening it happened several times.

Bruce talked about war, injustice, American hopes and promises. He spoke of playing at armories, and dance halls, and Bar Mitzvahs (yes, in his career Bruce played plenty of those). But he also spoke of stardom, and the loss of invincibility with his mortality on the horizon. At least in my view this was, perhaps, the logical equivalent to Bruce rocking the night. It was the literary Bruce. The writer. He "rocked" my heart. He was part Kerouac, part Langston Hughes, part Eugene O'Neill, part Steinbeck… but all Bruce.

He opened a pathway for a view into his soul and this audience loved it, every minute of it. I knew I did. I don't know if I've ever experienced anything quite like *Springsteen on Broadway*. I'm not a Bruce "true believer." That is, I can't recite every lyric of every song, and I haven't been to hundreds of his concerts, maybe five tops. I do however know that this show is, finally, what Bruce is. It is every bit as much as the inferno he creates when he plays "Thunder Road." He is, first, a writer, and those words and those phrases, observations, and reflections make him the greatest observer of the human condition in the rock 'n' roll business alive, maybe ever.

"It's not the time in your life, it's the life in your time," Bruce said.

After the show, my friend Kareem Abdul-Jabbar and our party

went to see Bruce backstage. I asked Kareem what he thought. "The way Bruce expressed the sense of mortality creeping up on us really got me," Kareem said. "You believe you are invincible, but slowly, as you age, and see your parents go, and your friends pass, and your body betray you, you realize that Bruce was right, that you can't be afraid of getting old. Old is good if you are gathering in life."

I told Bruce Springsteen how much the show affected me. I told him his words tore into me and his stories enlightened me, and then I said something else. Those words ignited me, and illuminated me, and moved me, and inspired me, and I wanted the night to go on forever.

"Aw thanks," Bruce said sheepishly. "I just wanna tell my story."

He told it well. What a story it was. And is.

The Rocket Man You Never Knew

An Elton John story:

I'm in Las Vegas interviewing Elton John. I'm not sure he remembers my name, but he tells me he is excited about doing our interview because he is such a sports fan. He claims he knew my show and watched *Up Close* every day! Oh, sure, all the rock legends are "sports fans." Yeah right, Elton. We start the interview.

He starts talking about Rafael Furcal!

"What are the Braves going to do with that young shortstop?" he asks. "When, I suppose, Marcus Giles is the more seasoned veteran?"

What? I couldn't believe it! He starts talking about Vinny Castillo and BJ Surhoff and starts asking me stuff about the Braves I didn't even know. I was blind-sided. Elton John was a serious Atlanta Braves fan!

"I used to watch the Braves on TBS when they were America's team owned by Ted Turner," he says. "See, I almost never leave my hotel on the road until sound check and show, so all I watched were Braves games and soaps. I fell in love with the Braves and I've been a massive fan for 25 years."

He goes on.

"When the Braves were in the playoffs regularly I used to have the games played low in my earpiece while I was onstage. *(!)* If the Braves won I'd be so happy, I'd perform an extra ten minutes. When they lost, and I heard Skip Caray in my ear, I'd be so upset that I'd cut the show short by a song or two. I guess it's unprofessional, but that was the truth. I love my Braves."

I think at first this is all a joke and that Elton was somehow briefed on what to say. But then he talks about Henry Aaron's record-breaking home run in 1974.

"I watched that on TV. And later I got to meet Henry and got a signed ball from him!"

I'm stunned. Years later I see Elton again at a MusicCares show in Los Angeles. He waves me over. It's not considered cool to go to a superstar's table at a function, but Elton John is waving me over and tells security to let me in.

"Remember I told you Furcal was going to be something special?" he asks. "Didn't think I wouldn't remember our conversation?"

Then he said, "Good to see you again, Roy."

He knew my name now!

Elton also knows tennis, World Cup soccer, and some auto racing. No basketball. He doesn't dig the NBA, NFL or boxing.

I talked to him about any regrets he had in his career.

"Only one thing," he said. "My time. All you really have is time. And my mom used to say, 'I don't want furs or cars or gifts from you, Reg (Reggie Dwight is his real name). I want you to spend time with me.'"

I thought about that line when Sir Elton John talked retirement and wanting to see his friends and family (what's left of them) and spend more time with his young children.

It's so true after all this time. Gigantic celebrities, all of them, are just people trying to find a way to a "normal life" if they can. Elton is someone who had a lot of demons early on, but he loves sports and people, and he really loved his mom and family. And now he'll be able to make the time for all of it.

Tell Them Now

Don't wait. Tell them now. Don't wait for it to be a eulogy. Don't delay and regret you never put the words together when they were here. Tell them that you are a better person for them having been in your life. That they inspired you, moved you to be something good and positive. That you learned something from them you couldn't have found without them. That they brought you the greatest gift, maybe something that you couldn't hold in your hand, but something that you can have in your heart and mind forever.

They made you more aware. More compassionate. Smarter. Wiser. Better. They ignited your humanity. Tell them.

The teacher who taught you something that wasn't easily found in any book. The lover or friend who made you more whole. The man or woman on the public service beat. The soldier, the fireman, the cop. The father who may have said silly things or acted goofy or had a bad temper and said things you wish he wouldn't at times, but taught you all those subtle life lessons. The mother who sometimes seemed overbearing and nosey, but whose light became part of you in the best of ways. Tell grandma, grandpa, uncle, aunt, brother, sister, niece, nephew. Tell the son or daughter.

Tell them.

Tell them now.

Tell the best friend you ever had, the one you might've taken for granted here or there or the one you just never got around to putting it into words for. That because of their presence you laughed harder, saw something in yourself that they showed you in their time here that made you feel safer, less alone, happier, more loved.

Every day, everywhere, there are people around you whose very presence in your life brought you the greatest gifts of all and you never really thanked them and never really told them. Tell them. Tell them now. Don't wait. Time isn't in a vacuum. It hurtles forward at an alarming and unrelenting pace. You will awaken one day and it will have passed. It will be letters never written, words never spoken.

Tell them. Tell them all. That you are a better man, a better woman ... just because they were here ... because they were a big part of your life. Tell them how much you love them, appreciate them, and honor them. Give gratitude easily, freely, without hesitation or fear because they won't be here forever. And neither will you.

Tell them.

Tell them now.

A Profile in Courage and Love

I consider George Will, the political commentator and academic, to be a friend. He wrote the foreword for my first book and was a frequent guest on my show. George and I share few if any political views, and that's more than fine. He's a lot more intelligent than I will ever be, and he's forgotten more than I will ever know about politics. We do share one unmistakable thing in common: baseball. We both love the game.

But there's a side to George that is rarely seen by the public. He's written about it here and there but mostly keeps it private, because he rightly cherishes his private life.

George Will has four children from two marriages. One of his kids is Jon ... or Jonny if you get to know him. I was lucky enough to meet Jonny a few times at baseball games and collectible shows. He's enthusiastic, knowledgeable about the game, and a real baseball fan.

He also happens to have Down syndrome.

About 400,000 Americans have Down syndrome, the most common genetic condition in the United States. It produces an array of challenges, including cognitive disability, delayed language and slow motor development.

Jon Will is 47 years old at this writing. That in itself is something of a miracle, because in 1960 a child born with the syndrome was only expected to live to the age of 10.

George Will is not an overtly sentimental man, at least not publicly. He is tart and critical of politicians and is intellectually consistent with his values without apology. But when the subject of Jon is mentioned something happens to George, and it is wonderful to see.

George Will becomes Jon Will's greatest supporter and biggest fan because, well, that's what loving dads are for their children. Writes George of his son, who was born on George's birthday in 1972:

Two things that have enhanced Jon's life are the Washington subway system, which opened in 1976, and the Washington Nationals baseball team, which arrived in 2005. He navigates the subway expertly, riding it to the Nationals ballpark, where he enters the clubhouse a few hours before game time and does a chore or two. The players, who have climbed to the pinnacle of a steep athletic pyramid, know that although hard work got them there, they have extraordinary aptitudes because they are winners of life's lottery. Major leaguers, all of whom understand what it is to be gifted, have been uniformly and extraordinarily welcoming to Jon, who is not."

I don't use the term "typically developing" in describing three of George's children in singling out Jon. Because George Will would tell you all his kids enhanced his life.

But Jonny IS different. His life is full of obstacles and hardships. These don't make him inferior, only different.

I've known many public figures who have children with Down syndrome. The former football Coach at Alabama, Gene Stallings, had a son named John Mark—Johnny— who was born with Down syndrome. Gene Stallings is 84 years old. Every year he hosts a golf tournament to raise money for a school for children with Down syndrome...and Johnny was there. He was always there.

When Stallings was fired as the Arizona Cardinals coach, he cried. Not because he'd lost his job, but because John worked for the Cardinals too… and he'd lost his job with his dad.

"He made my life richer, and I became more a more compassionate and empathetic man because of Johnny," Gene told me several years ago. Johnny passed away in 2010 at the age of 46.

Parents who have children with Down syndrome know better than anyone else that life can be harder, more challenging, and sometimes heartbreaking. But over the years almost all of them have told me that those children are special. More loving. More sensitive and kindhearted.

More rewarding to be around.

There's a time-honored quote from Down syndrome children:

I'm not "down".

I'm up.

I raise people up.

My smile is contagious.

My laugh is medicine for the heart.

My hugs are heavenly.

My heart is pure gold.

George Will is a decorated columnist and author. Gene Stallings won a national football championship at Alabama. Both would tell you that none of their accomplishments hold a candle to the blessing their children with Down syndrome has given them.

Unconditional love is the most powerful force in the universe. Parents of children with Down syndrome wouldn't change them for the world. They would just wish the world would change in how they look at them.

He said ... *What?*

It was a shock when Mike Tyson turned 50. Another one of those "hard-to-believe" moments. Tyson is many things to many people. He is the former heavyweight champion of the world, the youngest ever to claim the throne. He is also a convicted rapist, controversial author, actor, and celebrity icon.

I always got along with Mike. There are a ton of people who like him even with the obvious flaws and criminal record. Here's a funny and amazing story, and it's all true.

After Tyson knocked out Michael Spinks in 91 seconds of the first round on June 27, 1988, he stormed out of the ring with five of his corner men and entourage members. As he was running into the press room—not two minutes after knocking Spinks out cold --Tyson saw me in the middle of the hallway.

"Hey Roy, come over here," he said. I stopped and walked over to him. His entourage was pleading for Mike to go straight to the pressroom, but Mike wasn't having it. I assumed he was going to tell me how he just knocked out Spinks and that he was "the baddest man on the planet." Nope. He said this:

"Hey, I saw the show with your dad and you the other night. I had no idea your dad knew so much about boxing. Please give him my best and tell him that, okay?"

I was stunned. It was 11 o'clock at night. I called my father on a pay phone (*remember them?*). I woke him up. "Dad," I said. "I'm at the Tyson fight."

My father says, "That hoodlum should be in jail. He is a horrible person" (Tyson wouldn't be convicted of rape for another four years).

I said, "Pop, I just want to tell you something. Mike Tyson just walked up to me and told me he loved the show you did with me about boxing and wanted you to know he had no idea how knowledgeable you were about the sport."

Silence for a few seconds.

My father then said, "Well, you know, Mike is quite a warrior and champion."

Hysterical, bizarre moment in my career, but something close to a metaphor for Tyson: Champion. Convicted rapist. TV talk show regular. Celebrity. Unpredictable. And yes, agree or not, lovable, or popular in a menacing kind of way. I don't know many people I've met in my lifetime who are all of those things. Mike Tyson turned 50.

I can't believe it.

Nobility Itself

I always felt overmatched when I had Arthur Ashe on my show. Overmatched intellectually and in personal experiences, and over-matched in the depth and wisdom department. Arthur Ashe was a real hero to me, and he was 100% authentic in his commitment to social justice and civil rights. My youngest son carries his name as a tribute.

I'd always liked Arthur from the very beginning of my career in Miami. Thankfully he liked me too. He did interviews with me, a then 21-year-old kid who was "over his head" on Miami local TV. I didn't have his command of history and world politics. That's why I'd like to share this story.

One day in the early 90's, I happened to see Arthur at Doral where he was a consulting tennis advisor for the country club. He looked rail thin, maybe even sickly, but you don't tell your guests that. He agreed to come on my show. He knew something I did not, and the world did not. He had contracted the AIDS virus through a blood transfusion. He would reveal this publicly some six months later, but for this day he didn't let on.

I asked a question that I really wanted him to answer. "In all your travels," I asked, "what is the most painful realization you have about humanity?"

Arthur looked at me as if I knew his medical diagnosis. He said this: "I have come to the deeply painful and heartbreaking realiza-tion that in every culture, every continent, every ideology, someone has to beat up someone else. It doesn't matter the color, the religion, the politics. Someone has to be the bully, and it never changes."

I said, "Have you thought about that lately?"

Arthur said, "I think about it every day, with every moment passing for me."

Remember, he wasn't sure if I knew he had AIDS.

He continued. "In all the years of my travel and experience, I had hoped that humanity could rise above differences—racial, religious, economic, and political. We can't do it, or we haven't done it yet."

I was stunned by this statement and hoped he would add something inspiring, but he didn't.

"This planet will succeed or fail in its ability for people to find peace, friendship, and cooperation for all regardless of their differences. I am not optimistic we can rise above those differences."

I've never forgotten what he said that day. Here was a dying man who wrote, and spoke, and protested, and risked his life for change and social justice all his life, and finally admitted it was unlikely to happen in his lifetime. It was an honest but sad comment.

Before he died Arthur Ashe granted me one of his last, if not his last, interview. I asked him if he remembered his previous comment to me that day. He said, "Yes, I remember, Roy, and I wondered if you knew I was on borrowed time. Now my most pleasurable moments in life are being with my wife Jeanne, and my daughter Camera."

I asked him what specifically he enjoyed most. He said, "I love watching my 5 year-old eating a piece of chocolate cake. She goes at it with such joy and passion. It has to be the most amusing and most innocent thing I can see these days."

Arthur was dead less than 11 months later. That was more than 25 years ago. Arthur's daughter is a grown woman now. His wife Jeanne never remarried. Things haven't changed much down here, Arthur.

I wonder what he'd think about Donald Trump, but I'm pretty sure what he'd say. I'm sorry Arthur, but things aren't looking much better today.

Big Charles

Wesley Unseld was a great basketball player for his college team, Louisville (his home town too) and later with the then Baltimore Bullets. Wes was a physical force in the game, a great rebounder and outstanding defender. He's one of the NBA's 50 greatest players ever and a Hall of Famer. When he came on the show I was stunned at how much he resembled Muhammad Ali (who was also born and raised in Louisville), and I told him so. Wes confided to me something he didn't talk about much. But it stunned me. He was related to Ali and knew him all his life!

But the story that I love to tell is what Wes told me about his dad, "Big Charles," a mammoth figure with a lumberjack's build, the patriarch of the Unseld family. He was a force of nature, and actually built the family's home from scratch with his bare hands. He was a carpenter and a draftsman and he was an imposing, but deeply caring and loving human being.

I asked Wes what the greatest gift his father had given him was. He paused for a second and said this:

"The greatest gift my dad ever gave me and my brothers and sisters was simple. He loved my mother, and he loved her completely."

That got me.

Unseld continued:

"Wherever any of my brothers or sisters go in life, we learned how to love each other ... to love our family. I love my wife because my father showed me how to love."

These days, especially in today's tense and divisive climate, I think all of us should heed that story. We need to learn to love each other better, and surround ourselves with people who can give us examples of how to love. Surround yourself with people who know *how* to love with every fiber of their being. Surround yourself with people who are loved by others too, not for wealth, fame or status, but because of a basic quality of love from within their own heart.

Dr. Martin Luther King said the most profound thing in this quote:

"Darkness cannot drive out darkness: only light can do that. Hate cannot drive out hate: only love can do that."

Love people. Reject hate. Love yourself.

It's really pretty easy, pretty basic.

"Big Charles" knew how to do it ... and he passed the torch to future generations of the Unseld family.

Lassie Came Home

Here's a sweet story. When I was a kid I loved the TV show *Lassie* with Jon Provost and June Lockhart. I liked that it was very rural and had a soft edge to it, with nice music that appealed to an 8-year-old me. I also was madly in love with Lassie.

One day a commercial came on for Campbell's Soup, the show's sponsor: "If you send us six Campbell soup labels and one dollar, we will send you the official Lassie wallet with a Lassie Club Card."

I ate Campbell's Soup every day for a week and saved up enough for the wallet, and then I mailed it to Campbell's headquarters in Camden, New Jersey.

Every day I went to the mailbox. No wallet. A week went by, still no wallet. After a couple of months I was heartbroken. I lost hope. I was 8 years old and I thought I'd been ripped off and this hurt me. As a little boy it was the first disappointment from "grownups" that I can actually remember.

I never got the wallet.

Fast-forward 40 years later.

I do corporate speeches and presentations. One day I got a job for the Campbell's Soup Company. As I was being given a tour of the offices that day, me, at age 48, couldn't help thinking about that wallet. A weird thing came over me. I went to the woman at the front desk and explained my story. She wasn't sure if she should call security or not. Here was a grown man asking if he could get a Lassie Wallet. Finally, she just said, "Sir, I don't know what to tell you. I have no idea how you can get a Lassie Wallet." Oh well, you gotta try.

Years later I told a dear friend this story. She loved Lassie too, and both laughed at me and was touched by my innocence at the same time. On my next birthday I got a little package in the mail: It was a Lassie wallet in pristine condition with a "Lassie Fan Club Membership Card."

It's strange. I've gotten a lot of great gifts in my life, but probably none of them touched me like that gesture. I still love Lassie. And I love my wallet, even though I don't use it.

I keep it near me though to protect the innocence in me. And the 8 year-old in me is very, very happy.

I Never Played the Game

Arnold Palmer is gone. It's almost the end of the golden age of sports. He's gone with Ali, and Gordie Howe, and Musial and so many others whose grace and charm and appeal to the public transcended their mere athletic accomplishments.

Arnie was the "King" not just because of his 93 wins and four Masters titles, but because he connected with the public like few others in the history of sports. He was an everyman figure. Dashing, gritty, charismatic, and not complicated or controversial, Palmer was the first true television star in sports. In the early 60's it was "Arnie's Army" that banded together and turned golf tournaments, once quiet and intimate affairs, into something like a rock concert. But what I'll always remember about Arnie was his kindness and generosity, personal warmth and sense of humanity.

I had the honor of Arnold Palmer accepting the Roy Firestone award for our Los Angeles charity, West Coast Sports Associates. He couldn't have been more generous with his time and more helpful with every gesture, small or large. I was also honored to host several of his Bay Hill fundraisers which generated millions for his Arnold

Palmer Children's Hospital in Orlando. There will be other golfers, and maybe greater winners or players, but no one in the sport will ever be what Arnold Palmer was. He was the very face and soul and spirit of the sport, and he is irreplaceable.

I'm going to indulge myself with one personal Arnold Palmer story. He was a great man, and probably more importantly, he was a great guy. I don't want this to be about me, but it's kind of funny and he might have gotten a kick out of it if he'd heard it.

After the show in Maui, I was on the red-eye to host one of those Bay Hill events. After an especially taxing day I'd popped a sleeping pill—which didn't really do the job—and there I was pulling into the resort near Orlando at 4:15 a.m. without a wink of sleep. And still blitzed on the meds.

As I was checking in I heard a voice. "Hey, Roy, we've got a three-some. How 'bout making it a foursome?"

It was Arnold Palmer, at a table in the lobby with a couple of guys, asking me to play golf right then and there! I thought it was a hallucination. First, I'm not a golfer. I'm terrible. Playing with Arnie would be like me getting on the court with LeBron. Second, I didn't have any equipment. Third, I was so zonked I could barely form sentences. I looked at Arnold Palmer and said, "Arnie, thanks, but I can't. I'm wiped out and I have to get some sleep." The other two non-famous friends of Arnold looked at me like I'd lost my mind. *You're actually turning down Arnold Palmer for a round of golf??! Are you insane??! CEOs of top corporations pay hundreds of thousands of dollars to swat a golf ball with Arnold Palmer and you're waiving a free pass!* I put on the best smile I could muster and said, "Arnie, I'm really sorry. I can't play, but you should be happy 'cause I'm a really shitty golfer."

Palmer didn't miss a beat: "Roy, I play with the heads of companies all over the world. I play with nothing *but* shitty golfers."

I didn't play that round with Arnie. And to this day I can still picture the stunned look on those two other guys who went out to play with The King at 5 a.m. It's frozen in my memory. Of course, horrible golfer or not, I still have the regret, and I'll never stop kicking myself. That could have been the stupidest thing I didn't do in my entire life.

I TURNED DOWN THE CHANCE TO PLAY GOLF WITH ARNOLD PALMER.

Don Rickles & The Beatles

I grew up on Miami Beach. During my childhood there was one week when I can remember the town really buzzing. It was the third week of February, 1964. The Beatles were making their second ever live TV appearance in America on *The Ed Sullivan Show* at the Deauville Hotel, which was about a mile from my house. I remember how you couldn't get near the place. Also that week, Cassius Clay (Muhammad Ali's name before he changed it) was training for his fight with Sonny Liston. You may have seen the famous Beatles with Clay (Ali) photos, but there's another famous pairing of a celebrity with the Beatles that week and it's not as well known.

Don Rickles was becoming big as an insult comedian and was appearing at the Deauville too. One night the Beatles decided to go see the show. As Paul McCartney recalled it, Rickles (who rightfully earned his sarcastic nickname "Mr. Warmth") soon turned his acidic wit in the direction of the Fab Four.

"We were all on one table with our policeman buddy, our chaperone—we had this one bodyguard who came everywhere with us; he was a good mate and we often went back to his house—and Rickles started in on him: 'Hey, cop, get a job! What's this? Looking after the Beatles? Nice job you got there, man!' He went on, 'It's great. They just lie up there on the ninth floor in between satin sheets, and every time they hear the girls screaming they go, *Oooohh.*' We were not amused, as I recall. Very cutting. I like him now, but at first he was a bit of a shock."

Turns out, that "shock" drove the Fab Four to the door. They left the show well before it ended. Except that when the Beatles left, so did most of the rest of the audience.

Rickles recalled, "I loved the Beatles, but the truth is, I loved the packed houses they brought in because the Beatles were the hottest thing in show business. When they walked out that one night, I lost the rest of my audience too."

Rickles and individual members of the Beatles made up in later years. Ringo called him his favorite comedian.

Marvelous, Sugar and Frank

In April of 1987 I was ringside at the Sugar Ray Leonard-Marvin Hagler fight in Las Vegas. I was a pretty good friend of Ray's, and still am today. But I thought Marvin was going to kill him. Ray was two years younger than Marvin, didn't have even half the number of fights Marvin had and had "retired" from boxing for more than three years. Hagler was a brutal and vicious southpaw who demolished most every fighter he ever faced.

I was hoping Ray could just hold his own and turn in a respectable performance. In the first round I was astonished to see Leonard stand toe to toe with Marvin in a fight scheduled to go 12 (Ray insisted on a shorter fight and gave Marvin more money to agree). Leonard was the busier fighter, and even surprised Marvin with a clowning bolo punch or two. This infuriated Hagler. But as the first round ended, Leonard won the crowd over. The guy sitting in front of me in row four of ringside was taking photos. I didn't notice who it was, but he turned around after snapping a few and said (to no one in particular), "Kid's gonna win."

As he turned back I got a good look at his face. *It was Frank Sinatra!* Sinatra was a big fight fan. He'd done some boxing himself in his early days in Hoboken, New Jersey and also photographed the Ali-Frazier super fight in Madison Square Garden.

The fight went all 12 rounds. Leonard won a controversial decision, which to this day many people don't accept. As he was walking out after the decision was announced, Sinatra turned to our entire row and simply said, "Told ya."

The fight is over. The press conference is over and it's pitch black in the Caesars Palace parking lot. I see a lone figure coming toward me from a short distance. At first I'm afraid of being mugged. But then as I get closer I see who it is. *It's Marvin Hagler!*

"THEY TOOK IT AWAY FROM ME! TOOK IT AWAY! TOOK IT AWAY!" He keeps saying only that; he must have declared it ten times in a row. I think he was having some sort of post-fight breakdown or something. He doesn't even know who he was talking to. I don't try to identify myself but just watch him repeat the phrase over and over again, walking slowly into the shadows all by himself.

I've never forgotten that moment. Marvin never fought again. He went on to a brief acting career in spaghetti westerns. A few months later I told Ray that story. Ray looked at me and said, "Roy, *they* didn't take it away. *I* took it away."

Some people thought Marvin was robbed. I didn't. And Frank Sinatra hadn't either.

Wild About Harry

His name was Harry Chapin.

If you are old enough, you know he was a troubadour, a story-telling, folk-flavored performer who sold millions of records with songs like "Cats in the Cradle", "W.O.L.D.", and of course the near-mythic single "Taxi." Rather than talk about Harry as merely a great performing artist, I want to talk about his compassion, his astonishing selflessness, and his generosity.

Harry raised tens of thousands of dollars for the Performing Arts Foundation, the principal theatrical group on Long Island, and mobilized the business community to support the arts. He was a key participant in the creation of the Presidential Commission on World Hunger in 1977. In 1987 he was posthumously awarded the Congressional Gold Medal for his humanitarian work. He appeared in many benefit concerts for causes, including a campaign against world hunger, environmental and consumer issues and the Multiple Sclerosis Foundation. At one time, more than half his concerts were benefits.

One report quotes his widow saying soon after his death—"only with slight exaggeration"—that "Harry was supporting 17 relatives, 14 associations, seven foundations, and 82 charities."

Harry wasn't interested in saving money. He always said, "Money is for people," so he gave it away. Despite his success as a musician he left little money. It was difficult to maintain the causes for which he raised more than $3 million in the last six years of his life.

The Harry Chapin Foundation was the result. Since his death, it has now raised tens of millions of dollars for the poor, the hungry, the disenfranchised and the arts since, and it is still going strong today. No performer before him did as much for as many, and he ushered in an era for artists using their work for good. Artists like the late John Denver, Bono, Sting, James Taylor, Peter Gabriel, and many, many, more were inspired to donate their time and energy to make this planet more harmonious, more humane, and healthier and happier.

I never met Harry, though my closest friend in life knew him well. And though this friend is an "orthodox skeptic" about Hollywood and celebrities, he once said of Harry—without irony or sarcasm—that "he was the real deal."

On the day Harry died in a car accident in July of 1981, I was with my friend and his wife when he got the call. I'll never forget that moment. There were real tears, real loss, and deep sadness. Harry believed greatness wasn't as important as goodness, and were he alive today would be appalled at what he was seeing from our leaders and representatives. I believe Harry would have considered public office if not full-time public service; in fact, I'm sure of it.

This planet is better for his presence, and millions of people's lives are improved and bettered from Harry's efforts. What greater accomplishment is there for a human being?

One of the lyrics that still inspires and resonates for me is Harry's song "I Wonder What Would Happen to this World."

"Oh if a man tried
To take his time on Earth
And prove before he died
What one man's life could be worth
I wonder what would happen to this world?"

Those lyrics are written on Harry's epitaph. Miss you, Harry. Wish you were here.

A Christmas Story

Here's a wonderful Christmas music story. Frank Pooler was the choir director at Cal State Long Beach. In 1946, just after the war, he was stationed in Germany, and during holiday time missed his fiancée. Frank wrote a longhand poem to her called "Merry Christmas, Darling." It had no melody.

He and his fiancée would not marry, and Pooler married another woman who later passed. But one night years later Pooler was having dinner at a local restaurant (since his wife passed he didn't eat home much). There was an older lady across the dining area. She looked familiar, so he asked her name: she turned out to be the old sweetheart he'd been engaged to during WWII. They both could hardly believe it. Needless to say they continued their meal together that night, and he proceeded to tell her the story about that long-ago lonesome poem, "Merry Christmas, Darling." His old flame was moved and suggested that he put it to music. They both finished dinner with a tear and a smile in their eyes.

A few years later, in 1966, Pooler met CSLB music student Richard Carpenter. He asked Carpenter to come up with a melody for the poem. Carpenter wrote the melody and had his sister Karen sing it… and the rest is history. This song, particularly the vocal part, is one of the greatest holiday songs ever. To me, next to "Superstar," it's Karen's best recording ever. Listen to her sing it and remember this backstory. Merry Christmas one and all.

Dad

Sometimes when I see a great play on a baseball field, I am moved to call him. Then I remember he isn't here anymore. When I see some old movie star like William Holden, Spencer Tracy, or Humphrey Bogart, I think of him.

But he's not here to tell me about William Holden, or Tracy, or any star or singer from his era I'd be curious to ask him about. Wikipedia works, but in a way it's too handy and quick. It doesn't have the insight, humor, charm, and storytelling panache my dad had.

It's been years now, but he's still with me every day. He's with me when I hear K.D. Lang sing a song. Or Karen Carpenter or Sinatra or Nat King Cole. He's with me when I think of Jack Lemmon, one of his favorite actors. He's still inside my heart when music moves me, or good writing inspires me, because he knew great music and he was a terrific writer.

My dad wouldn't have liked much of what's on the internet and social media. He was well mannered, graceful, and didn't engage in backbiting or with mean-spirited people.

His opinion mattered to him. He didn't need confirmation from anyone else.

My dad loved most sports, but baseball was his way of connecting best with me.

I could mention any player today, and he'd usually just smile and say two words: "Willie Mays." He lived through the Depression, and multiple wars, and his own longings and some financial heartbreak. But he also regaled me with stories of the beautiful, heroic, funny, poetic and elegant things that made up his world.

He could make me laugh like no one else before or since, and I was the person who most made him laugh. I took that responsibility seriously. He had a hearty and generous laugh, and so did his wife, my mom. They both had laughs that could be described as sunny and fluorescent. They were big laughers. Loud laughers. They laughed often and easily.

They were married for close to 60 years, and when the end came for my mom, he couldn't go on. His light was gone. Part of his spirit and soul was extinguished.

My dad was an expert on many things.

He knew Gershwin, and Rogers and Hammerstein and a million songs and songwriters.

He could talk about boxing in the thirties, and movies—God, how he loved movies—and he never used the word "films," only "movies." He talked about movies with Jimmy Stewart and Grace Kelly and Robert Mitchum, and Gable and Hepburn, and a ton more, especially Jack Lemmon.

And he loved his teams, too. The Giants came first, and, later, the Dolphins, Marlins and Miami Heat.

He wasn't a handy person. His eyes would glaze over when he had to look at a manual or anything technical. He never picked up a shovel or a rake. He had no idea what a garden was. But he could describe in detail why Ella Fitzgerald was America's greatest singer, and why Red Barber, the Dodgers announcer before Scully, was a lyrical and graceful baseball broadcaster, like Vin would become.

He never dismissed my love for rock and roll even though he pretty much despised it personally. When John Lennon was killed and my heart was shattered, I remember him hand writing and mailing me a letter—which I still have to this day—about loss and tragedy and grief and human suffering. In that four-page letter he touched my heart and soothed my despair.

I've said it before and I'll say it again. I never was, and never will be, the man my father was. He was smart, and compassionate, and wise and true...and also flawed. I think I learned to love his flaws as much as I loved his virtues.

I remember I always had him as a guest on my show on Father's Day. Some people thought this was corny, or even inappropriate. But now there's a TV show where the host's father appears on the show every day, mostly for laughs.

We laughed together over the phone. I wish I could laugh again with pop, about something stupid, or about our political car wreck today, or just about something Richard Pryor said on TV. I wish he were here.

If you had a dad like I did and he is gone, try and hold the memories close and keep them. If he is alive and you love him, tell him that. He'll be happy to hear it.

If you're lucky, you really only get one dad. I was extraordinarily lucky. Happy Father's Day, dad.

A Wizard: A True Star

I'm frequently asked what was my best interview I ever conducted. I've done about 5,000 of them, and it's hard to state definitively which was "best." Some of the most memorable were Lyle Alzado, Mickey Mantle, Magic Johnson, Bill Walton, and Hubie Brown. But the most in-depth, most heavily-researched, and to me, the most unforgettable was of someone who is not an athlete or sportsperson in any way.

It was a 2010 interview with rock legend Todd Rundgren.

First, a bit of a background. The year was 1972, and I was an 18-year-old kid with a friend named "Leapin" Larry Greene, and both of us had listened to a brilliant album called *Something/Anything?* by Todd Rundgren. On most of it, Todd played all the instruments. He wrote the music and produced and engineered it too. I couldn't

believe how many hits were on that album, including "Hello, It's Me," "I Saw the Light," and the extremely underrated "It Wouldn't Have Made Any Difference."

Larry Greene turned me on to that record in our college dorm with tremendous Sennheiser headphones. I was hooked on Todd forever. Larry and I were pals and I told him, "Someday I'll interview this guy." We both laughed.

Larry and I worked together in radio, TV, and other productions. In 2002, after 9/11, Larry Greene was tragically killed in a helicopter accident in the Persian Gulf. I was devastated. I wanted to tell Todd Rundgren, whom I'd never met personally, about Larry, and asked him if he would record a video honoring the memory of my friend for his memorial.

I somehow got his number in Hawaii, and Todd, who really wasn't much of a sports fan, picked up the phone and was touched by my story. He recorded a special video for the memorial and I will never forget the gesture.

Fast-forward almost a decade. I called Todd Rundgren's office and asked if I could interview Todd for a TV special. Not only did his office agree, but they offered as much time as I needed in an interview before a live audience in Todd's hometown of Philadelphia.

Todd is a brilliant artist. He's produced hundreds of hit records—including all of his own—and engineered or produced everyone from Janis Joplin, Badfinger, Meatloaf and Psychedelic Furs to Hall & Oates, Grand Funk and many others. And of course he had his own career of top of the charts hits and live shows.

We set the interview up at the famed Franklin Museum in Philadelphia. At the time Todd rarely did extended interviews and was notorious for being wary of the media.

He certainly was smarter and quicker than most interviewers, and I knew that. Prior to our meeting—for two solid months—I researched and pre-interviewed everyone from Ann Wilson of Heart, Darryl Hall of Hall & Oates, to Paul Schafer of *Late Night with David Letterman*, and dozens more. They were all in awe of Todd. I never worked harder for an interview preparation in my entire career.

The night of the interview came and I was actually nervous because I felt overmatched. But Todd came out and somehow connected with me and gave me one of the greatest interviews in my career. He told me some stunning things. His greatest musical influences, he said, were Leonard Bernstein, Burt Bacharach, Gilbert and Sullivan, and, believe it or not, Tony Bennett!

He told stories of his career from the time he was a teenager with his early bands, and how he engineered *Pearl*, the album Janis Joplin was working on when she died. Todd told incredible stories about George Harrison and John Lennon and admitted Lennon's killer was also looking to kill him!

He talked of his career and his family. He talked of regret and loss. Most people don't know that Todd raised actress Liv Tyler as a small child, when her real father (*Aerosmith*'s Steven Tyler) was addicted to heroin, and he talked of the heartache of losing her in a custody battle. But Todd is a great father to three boys, Rex, Randy, and Rebop.

The interview went on and on and Todd couldn't have been more candid, accessible, and insightful. The audience loved it and, without any interruptions, the interview lasted—get this—three and a half hours!

I had never interviewed anyone like Todd before, someone who was as wise as he was accomplished. When he was told the interview lasted three and a half hours, he was shocked. "It seemed like maybe an hour or so," he said.

After the interview Todd took me out to his favorite Philadelphia deli and gave me a signed electric guitar. I still cherish the guitar in my music room. I believe Todd Rundgren is easily worthy of the Rock and Roll Hall of Fame, but he told me that if nominated he wouldn't accept or attend.

He is one of the great figures in rock history, but never went out of his way to write hit songs, even though they came easily to him. He told me that night, "While I'm not opposed to commercial success, when I doubt, I err on the side of art."

Todd still tours, writes, performs, and produces great records, and he even tours with Ringo Starr's band. I'll never forget that interview and I'll also never forget the guy who introduced me to Todd: my buddy "Leapin" Larry Greene.

There has never been a better guest at the other end of my microphone. Todd truly is a wizard. A genuine star.

The Greatest Remembered

He was outrageous. He was talented. He was brash and bold. He was controversial before any athletes were all of those things in public. He was loved. He was despised. He was a hero. Some called him a traitor or a coward. He was the single most important athlete in my lifetime and he was a friend. He meant so much to me in my life and career.

He was the first person I ever interviewed and he remembered it almost every time I saw him, even until he couldn't speak anymore. Muhammad Ali was perhaps the most famous athlete of all time, but he was also a man who stood up for black people. He did it loudly and without fear in a time when black people were getting shot for speaking up.

He refused to be drafted into a war he didn't believe in and he lost three-and-a-half years in the prime of his career because of principle. Many hated him then. Many called him anti-American.

Few feel that way anymore.

He was theater and skill, but he was also dignity, humor and confidence along with some arrogance, but that was mostly theater as well. Ali always told me he was an actor. When I had a bit part in the first movie about his life, a movie called *The Greatest*, he showed he could act. Even though he played himself, he played the part well.

Who else could do it better anyway?

Ali's death saddened all kinds of people, especially people who once loathed him. Now sometimes when I travel, I hear people say things like, "Man, I hated that s.o.b. in the sixties, but I love him so much now."

George Foreman tells me he loves him. His voice chokes when he tells me Ali was his friend, even after Ali beat him in one of the most ignominious beat-downs ever in 1974: the famed "Rumble in the Jungle."

I'm grateful Ali was in my life. He made such a profound impact on me, but no words can aptly describe what he meant to this planet. He gave the poor inspiration. He gave the disenfranchised hope and joy. He gave the rest of us quite a show.

No one will ever again be to sports what Ali was. He was a showman. He was a warrior.

He could barely read beyond a fifth-grade level, yet he was an athletic genius and one of the wisest and most clever people I've ever met.

The final bell has tolled. He showed us how to fight both in and out of the ring. For all its tragedy and hate and horror, Ali made this planet better a little bit at a time. He uplifted people. He did it every day in large and small ways.

He does it still.

Good Jerry/Bad Jerry

The death of Jerry Lewis hit me hard. For me as a kid, he was, indeed, the clown prince of comedy. Jerry Lewis was the center of my comedy universe. He was wild, unpredictable, an anarchist, a threat to grownups and people in authority. I felt as a little boy that he was "the kid" in an adult's body that represented a push against convention and mediocrity.

He got his start in 1946 alongside Dean Martin, performing on television and radio shows and in movies before they parted ways in 1956. Lewis went on to star in, produce, and direct an array of films. He hosted his own telethon for decades that raised millions of dollars for research for Muscular Dystrophy.

And then society began to change. First, the biggest comedy star in the world—the guy who defined madcap slapstick humor—ran into an era when satire, wit, and parody became popular and unhinged. Loud, chaotic comedies were rejected by the press and the public.

Then he was ridiculed for using his telethons as some kind of self-congratulatory platform for his own narcissism. Jerry was parodied, discredited, mocked, and marginalized. But the people who loved him for what he was never stopped loving him.

I was one of them.

I'm quite aware of his disgusting, boorish, "suck-air-out-of-the-room" side. His own son Gary Lewis, who later had a run of fame with his band, *Gary Lewis and The Playboys*, said he was the most abusive, mean-spirited, and tyrannical father any child could ever have.

Even though I'm sure this was true, I didn't want to hear about it. Jerry was still my comedy hero. Of course, we are all aware of his nasty spats with the press, talk show hosts, and even fans. During one show, I saw him go after a fan who simply asked him if he could do an impression of him for Jerry.

None of that really affected how I felt about him. I had a show called *Up Close,* and before that *Sports Look*, and frequently we would have entertainers who loved sports come on.

We had nearly everyone—from Jerry Seinfeld and George Carlin to Robert Klein, Don Rickles and scores more. Just about every one of my comedy guests admired or was inspired by Jerry Lewis. One day I was sitting in my office checking my phone messages. I got a call from a man claiming to be "Jerry Lewis."

"Roy," the man said, "this is Jerry Lewis. I'm a huge sports fan and I'd love to come on your show."

I thought it was a prank call.

So I returned the call and it was the real Jerry. For the next half hour, Jerry Lewis was talking to me on the phone like we'd been

friends all our lives. He talked about his love of the Dodgers, his friendship with ballplayers and fighters. He told me about his rounds of golf with JFK and Joe Louis and how his stage name was supposed to be Joe Lewis, not Jerry Lewis. And then he came on my show.

ESPN was gracious enough to allow me to have two episodes with Jerry to talk about his many experiences in sports, including a classic story of how he bet on Buster Douglas to beat Mike Tyson and made a fortune.

Jerry knew I liked to perform on stage, a fact that some people in my profession mocked, dismissed, and sometimes ridiculed. Jerry somehow knew this.

He told me something I will never forget and I will take to the grave: "Roy, never apologize for doing something you love to do. If you're funny, be funny. If you like to sing, Goddammit, do it. You don't have to answer to anyone for your passion."

And then he said it.

"One day you'll probably appear in Las Vegas, and when you do I'll send you a telegram."

I laughed it off. A few years later in 1990, I co-headlined at the Golden Nugget in Las Vegas with Lou Rawls. In the dressing room before the show, I got a telegram. It was from Jerry.

"Don't ever apologize and don't let anyone see you sweat. Good luck and congratulations. Your pal, Jerry."

Many of you couldn't stand him, or outgrew him, or rejected him. But many of you laughed and were thrilled and entertained by him. I was always one of you.

In my life, there was Jerry, and there was everyone else in the comedy business. So thanks, Jerry. Thanks for the good work. For the laughs. For the movies. Thanks for the pep talk.

When Jerry died I lost a big part of my youth and a big inspiration in my life. Crazy Jerry, egotistical Jerry, nasty Jerry, kind Jerry, smart Jerry, charitable Jerry. Funny Jerry. They are all Jerry.

And I loved him ... and always will.

Bruce's Real Boss

If your mom is still with you, cherish her, hug her, look in her eyes, and tell her you love her. You won't always have your mom around.

Some remembrances of a self-proclaimed "Momma's boy."

Recently he said of her:

Truthfulness, consistency, professionalism, kindness, compassion, manners, thoughtfulness, pride in yourself, love within and fidelity to, commitment, joy in working ... a never-say-die thirst for life.

She was my protector. How did she express her frustrations? With appreciation for the love and home she had, a gentle kindness to her children, and love for more work. My mother would read romance novels, and swoon to the latest hits on the radio. My mother could make merry conversation with a broom handle. She always had my back.

When I got hauled down to the police station for some minor offenses, she was always there to take me back home. She took me to my countless ballgames. She got me my first electric guitar, encouraged my music, and fawned over my early creative writing.

This "Momma's boy" is the first to admit it, and it is a proud, unashamed proclamation.

His mom celebrated her 93rd birthday in 2018, and to honor it this "Mama's Boy" danced with his mom again. He's done it every year for decades, no matter how big he gets—and he's very big—and he's still his Mama's baby.

The mom's name is Adele. The "Mama's boy" is Bruce Springsteen.

Maybe not every mom "gets it right." Some can frustrate us or in-

71

furiate us, and there may be some days when mom breaks our heart. But if your mom is still here, let her know, if you can, that you are whole because of her. That she listened when you needed an ear. That she spoke when you needed a talking to. That her spirit and love and soul will stay with you for the rest of your life. That's the mother's gift.

So, like Bruce, if you are able and she is here, ask her to dance with you.

Dads are great too, but you are only here because your mom brought you here. Nurtured you. Taught you. Loved you.

Dance with your mom or remember her as the light in your life.

There's really only one mom. She's the only one you'll ever need.

The Sting of Fame

If you haven't watched *The Zen Diaries of Garry Shandling*, you should. It's an absolutely brilliant piece of work by Judd Apatow.

One thing that struck me was Shandling's deep friendship with Tom Petty. For two enormously successful and beloved entertainers, almost nothing could settle their restlessness, their unhappiness, and longing. They died almost exactly a year apart, at exactly the same age, both from heart embolisms. Petty, by all accounts, had a happy family, and his kids adored him. And yet he was a chain smoker who had many different drugs in his system at the end of his life, including fentanyl, Oxycontin, and antidepressants.

They had different histories and upbringings of course, but they were, in the end, similar spirits. For all their good work there seemed to be enormous pain in their lives. Garry was a deeply restless soul who mistrusted his success and had a kind of PTSD all through his life, some theorize because he never really got over his older brother's death. Both were giants in their fields of entertainment. But you wonder if they'd been, say, in retail sales, or worked in an office, or anything mundane like that, if the flames of unhappiness and uncertainty would have engulfed them in the same way.

I didn't know either of these people, though I had met Shandling a few times. I just don't know, but it seems fame is, for so many, a demon in itself. Fame becomes an elusive and ever-demanding thing that needs to be fed. Nothing ever seems to be enough, and the angst, pressure, and unhappiness seem to be almost overwhelming for so many. I think both people were fine human beings, with great qualities, but they were clearly troubled.

I'm not trying to pass judgment on either man, but success and fame may not be such a bargain. When people say, "Hey, you've got tens of millions of dollars, a fleet of cars, a massive home, adulation and a body of work. What's the problem?"

It's this.

The work. The money. The attention. The affection.

Fame has insatiable demands, and almost nothing can easily assuage the anxiety that comes with it. It's never enough. It's an artificial life. For many, it's a sad life.

And yet, most people would love to be in their shoes.

"Just shut up, do the work, take the check, and go home."

"Stop with the indulgence of the tortured artist."

But for so many, it's just not possible.

Both Sides Now

She attended the James Taylor concert at the Hollywood Bowl last night, sitting discreetly at the back of the Garden section in a wheelchair wearing a ball cap and wrapped in warm clothing. Most people didn't notice her. Lots wouldn't have recognized her if they had.

Joni Mitchell doesn't make music anymore. That simple fact is sad enough, because at 74, had she not smoked for 61 years, she still might have been able to sing her sweet and beautiful songs, like "Both Sides Now," "Big Yellow Taxi," "Woodstock," "Help Me," and "A Case of You" somewhere on some stage on some tour.

But it wasn't to be.

Her voice has been ravaged, and her life tormented by battles with polio, paranoia, and her struggle with a rare and controversial disease called Morgellons. Joni Mitchell remains, to me, perhaps the greatest singer/artist/songwriter of the 20th century, or at least near the top of the elite.

Yet she welcomes obscurity and shuns publicity after a near-death stroke that many believed would be her final curtain. Joni Mitchell has lived with much heartbreak. She abandoned her career for two years and "cried for a year" after a bad marriage and giving her daughter away for adoption.

When she reunited with her daughter about a decade ago, Joni also became an instant grandparent, and the joy washed away much of the sorrow and guilt.

Her friends visit her, and she still paints, brilliantly, but not with the frequency she once did. Her artistry is so diverse and her work so varied on canvas and acrylic that she might have been a more acclaimed artist as a painter or sculptor.

She grants no interviews but remains a passionate environmentalist, only speaking publicly on that subject. Last night she was escorted slowly and quietly in her wheelchair and few, if any, paid attention to her. By any standard this woman has led an amazing creative and productive life. But there is still sadness in seeing her as something like the self-portrait she painted that was inspired by her hero, Vincent Van Gogh.

She is alone, but not lonely, quiet but not muted, challenged but not defeated.

There is a special place in my heart for Joni Mitchell. Millions have that place too. No doubt she visited with her former lover and friend James Taylor after the show, or before it, and she might have recalled old times, music, art, or just engaged in small talk.

Joni Mitchell is alive. She's not what she was, but she is alive and trying to live a mainly reclusive life free from pain, anguish, and illness. Cherish her. Remember her while she is here.

A Joni Mitchell public sighting is rare, like seeing some endangered species, but her art and her music will outlive her and remain vibrant and alive for hundreds of years.

Hope you enjoyed the show, Joni.

We certainly enjoyed yours. Stay well.

Don't Make Me Cry, Roy

Almost every single day for the last 22 years, someone comes up to me at an airport, or diner, or gas station, and says, "Don't make me cry, Roy."

It's a reference to my scene in *Jerry Maguire*, the Academy Award-winning movie starring Tom Cruise. I was on camera for about ninety seconds, but the now famous utterance (not really made with those words) by Cuba Gooding Jr. has lived with me since 1996, the year the film was released. Here is some interesting background info about the scene and my line.

First, the original Rod Tidwell—played so brilliantly by Gooding Jr.—was to have been Dennis Rodman, who turned down the role. (I guess he was focusing on his dream to perform Shakespeare on Broadway). I was going to be played by someone else too, but when director Cameron Crowe called my ESPN office looking for "a Roy Firestone type," he was told that the "real Roy Firestone" was available. I was worried that the "real Roy Firestone" wouldn't be believable.

I got the job. I was sent the script. I barely read it. I figured the scene, like most of the scenes I've done in movies, would be cut and never make the final edit. I was wrong.

When I walked onto the set at Sony in Culver City, Tom Cruise was playing catch with a kid I thought had to be his son. It wasn't his son. Cruise was developing a relationship with the child actor Jonathan Lipnicki, the boy who nearly stole the film as the son of Cruise's girlfriend (played by Renee Zellweger).

77

Cruise was on set for every moment of my scene. He was a terrific guy, very friendly, and a huge sports fan who wanted to talk sports with me all day. He introduced me to a guy named Cuba (Gooding Jr.). I had never heard of the name because he was relatively unknown. I thought Cruise said he was *from* Cuba, so I asked Gooding Jr. where in that country he was from. We straightened that out quickly.

Remember, I'd only skimmed the script, and hardly knew the story line. We ad-libbed about 80% of the scene. My own contribution was the "tragic bass fishing accident." We did two takes. The first, where Cuba Gooding hugs me, nearly ended in tragedy. When he stretched across the table to grab me, he pushed my rolling chair and I nearly fell off backwards. But two alert grips jumped into action and saved me. We did the second take: it was a keeper.

Cuba Gooding Jr. produced *real tears* in his eyes on both takes! That stunned me, but that's acting, I guess. We did the take and the movie was released. Cuba Gooding Jr. won the Academy Award for best supporting actor, and I got to add "appeared in an Academy Award-winning film" to my resume.

But that's not my greatest takeaway from this story. Three years later, while in Liverpool, I was at a party where a rock icon walked up to me.

"You're the guy who makes people cry!" he said. "What's your name, again?"

"Roy," I said.

"Don't make me cry, Roy!" he blurted out.

That rock icon was Paul McCartney. *That* almost made *me* cry!

Big Cheeks

On a different note, from time to time I love to share the "rest of the story" in pop culture. This one is great:

"Big cheeks" was a grandson of slaves, a boy who was born in a poor neighborhood of New Orleans known as the "Back of Town." His father abandoned the family when the child was an infant. His mother became a prostitute and the boy and his sister had to live with their grandmother. Early in life he proved to be gifted with music, and with three other kids sang in the streets of New Orleans. His first gains were coins that were thrown to them.

A Jewish family named Karnofsky, who had emigrated from Lithuania to America, had pity for the 7-year-old boy and brought him into their home. Initially giving him "work" in the house, they cared for and fed this hungry child. There he remained. He lived and slept in this family's home where, for the first time in his life, he was treated with kindness and tenderness. When he went to bed, Mrs. Karnovsky sang him a Russian lullaby that he would sing with her. Later he learned to sing and play several Russian and Jewish songs.

Over time this boy became the adopted son of this family. The Karnofskys gave him money to buy his first musical instrument, as was the custom in Jewish families. They sincerely admired his musical talent. Later, when he became a professional musician and composer, he used these Jewish melodies in compositions, such as "St. James Infirmary" and "Go Down Moses."

The little black boy grew up and wrote a book about this Jewish family who had adopted him in 1907. In memory of this family and until the end of his life, he wore a Star of David and said that in this family, he had learned "how to live real life and determination."

You might recognize his name. This little boy was called Louis "Satchmo" Armstrong. Louis Armstrong proudly spoke fluent Yiddish! And "Satchmo" is Yiddish for "Big Cheeks."

And I'll bet you did not know any of this.

Teacher and Pupil

We honored Kareem Abdul-Jabbar at our 22nd annual WSA Roy Firestone Award dinner at the Westin Bonaventure Hotel in Los Angeles. In preparation for our live on-stage interview with Kareem, I read his wonderful book about his friendship and relationship with Coach John Wooden. It's called *Coach Wooden and Me*.

This book is moving, inspiring, surprisingly warm and loving, and it shows Kareem in a completely different light. I've known Kareem for 40 years and have always enjoyed our friendship, and though he has never been Mr. Congeniality, I believe most of his problem (or the public's) is that he is deeply shy and distant to strangers. Yes, he has also made some mistakes, which he acknowledges in the book, but his commentary about his half-century friendship with Wooden is powerful and candid.

One of the lines in the book is this:

"I wish I had a time machine and I could go back to kick my younger self's ass."

Kareem writes about his spiritual awakening in his conversion of Islam, which he never felt had anything to do with politics and everything to do with spirituality. He writes of Wooden:

"I never heard him utter an unkind word about anyone in the 50 years I knew him."

And then there's this extraordinary passage:

"In the final days of his life, I looked at this shrunken 98 year-old with his thick glasses and his large jug ears, and I had a tenderness for him that I had taken for granted. I had modeled myself after him in so many ways and I was still learning how deep his influence ran. I realized that in all my writings about

black history, politics, and pop culture, it had one theme: making the playing field even so that everyone had the same opportunities, or, as Coach might say, "No one eats unless we all eat."

John Wooden would be deeply proud of his *student* first, and athlete second.

The Kick of the Year

In sports all the time we hear phrases like "court vision" or "seeing the whole field." But what if you can't see at all?

Blind since the age of 12, Jake Olson had at best a remote shot at college football. But the long snapper proved any doubters wrong when in September of 2017, he took the field for the University of Southern California and helped the Trojans make an extra point.

Olson's efforts put USC up 49-31 over Western Michigan in the fourth quarter, but the message sent by Olson—who'd joined the team in 2015—was far more significant. "There's a beauty in it," Olson told reporters after the game (via the *Los Angeles Times*' Bill Plaschke). "If you can't see how God works things out, then I think you're the blind one."

Olson was playing in his first regular season game. His big chance came after Marvell Tell III returned an interception for the game's final touchdown. Olson jogged onto the field with one hand on the shoulder of holder Wyatt Schmidt. When the kick by Chase McGrath was good, Trojan players danced and cheered and fans hugged. The "perfect snap" was, as Coach Clay Helton put it, "beyond words."

Frank Was Here

When I was bat boy for the Baltimore Orioles in Miami, things didn't start in the clubhouse till someone said "Frank is here." "Frank" of course was Frank Robinson, future Hall of Famer, one of baseball's greatest players ever, and the leader of the team. There were great names in that locker room, and a few would also someday be Hall Of Famers - Brooks Robinson, Jim Palmer, later Eddie Murray, and of course manager Earl Weaver.

But there was only one "Frank".

Frank came "here," to Baltimore, in 1966. He was traded away after the Cincinnati Reds' GM called him "an old 30." Frank would use that comment to motivate him, empower him. "When I saw him double down the right field line on the first day of spring training," Jim Palmer told Dick Hall, "we just won the pennant with that guy." He wasn't wrong. That year Robinson won the Triple Crown and led the Orioles to their first world championship.

As a ballplayer Robinson had few peers. Mantle was the bigger name and more beloved. Clemente was more graceful and elegant. Musial a better hitter. Mays and Aaron were more complete players. But Frank Robinson was something that those others were not: He was a fierce warrior.

When Frank Robinson walked into that locker room you could feel it. "Frank's here," yelled Paul Blair whenever he arrived. You knew who was in charge. Who assumed immediate command.

Frank was funny, sarcastic, acerbic, critical, uncensored, wise, and a true baseball sage. Earl Weaver, who confronted almost anyone, would never confront Frank. Weaver knew you don't mess with a warrior.

Frank Robinson's statistics were among the greatest in baseball history, but mere numbers can't define the leadership, authority, and influence this man had. No one else was Most Valuable Player in both the National and American leagues. No one else was Manager of the Year in both leagues. Frank Robinson was the first black manager in major league baseball, and he homered in his first at bat as a player-manager too.

He was a lion of a man.

There's an old sports cliché: "He came to play." Frank Robinson came to WIN. Frank was a figure who led, influenced, empowered, and inspired his teammates to take it all.

I remember the game when he hit the longest home run at Memorial Stadium; and the game when he hit TWO grand slams, the catch falling into the right field stands in New York.

But no one moment defines Frank Robinson better than beating the tag at home plate for the winning run in game 6 of the 1971 World Series. It was a metaphor for the player he was.

Frank Robinson was determined and aggressive and would not be denied. In this last World Series he would ever play in, he played that game like he knew he'd never have another chance.

Like the legendary predecessor who shared his last name, Jackie Robinson, Frank was strong-willed, courageous, stubborn, and single-minded. Like Jackie, he broke down barriers, pushed convention, and demanded to be respected and heard.

Talent was only part of it. Will was certainly most of it. There was a fire that burned within him and it erupted onto the field. Out there he brawled with Eddie Mathews. He slid hard on the base paths, taking all he endured. He suffered as a black man in baseball in the 50's and early 60's, exorcising his demons on the field of play.

He challenged teammates. He insulted teammates. He made them laugh and he made them competitively angry. He was a critic, and advocate and activist for his teammates and the game of baseball to do better. He offended some… and uplifted many.

Once, when he was Giants manager, he went to the mound to ask for the ball from the pitcher he was pulling. Jim Barr "flipped" it to him. Robinson grabbed Barr and snarled, "Don't you EVER flip a ball to me again… or I'll knock you on your ass right here in front of everyone."

Robinson demanded respect, and like Jackie, he didn't much care if you liked him or not. You WOULD respect him.

I can't say Frank Robinson was an easy man. He led a hard life in his youth, never knew his father, lived in poverty, and shared injustice with high school basketball teammates Bill Russell (yes, THE Bill Russell) Curt Flood, and Vada Pinson.

When he came to Baltimore he couldn't live in any white areas. Brooks Robinson helped him find a home for his family, and Frank never forgot Brooks' kindness and help. When he lay dying, Brooks called him and the two chatted with mutual respect and gratitude.

Frank Robinson was a force of nature. He never stepped back. He never stepped away from a challenge.

I saw his first at bat as an Oriole in his first spring training game. On the first pitch he hit a ball over the clock at Miami Stadium about 500 feet away.

The Orioles had arrived. "Frank was here." His loss to baseball is profound.

There were greater players, but not many. There weren't many who had a greater impact on the game. His like will never be seen again.

He was one of a kind.

"Frank WAS…here."

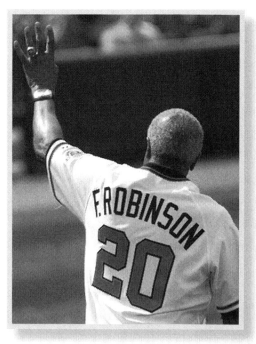

A Hero's Hero

At precisely 9:02 on the morning of April 19, 1995, an ex-Army soldier and security guard named Timothy McVeigh parked a rented Ryder truck in front of the Alfred P. Murrah Federal Building in downtown Oklahoma City. He was about to commit mass murder.

Inside the vehicle was a powerful bomb made from a deadly cocktail of agricultural fertilizer, diesel fuel and other chemicals. McVeigh got out, locked the door, and hurried to a getaway car. He ignited one timed fuse, then another.

Within moments the surrounding area looked like a war zone. A third of the building had been reduced to rubble, with many floors flattened like pancakes. Dozens of cars were incinerated and more than 300 nearby buildings were damaged or destroyed.

The human toll was still more devastating: 168 souls lost, including 19 children, with several hundred more injured. It was the worst act of homegrown terrorism in the nation's history.

As she sat at her hospital switchboard beginning her day, nurse Tammy Aikman didn't know her life was about to be changed forever. Suddenly the switchboard turned into a constellation of ringing bells and blinking lights. Hundreds, maybe thousands of families were calling all at once to find out if their husband, wife, or child was dead or alive.

Tammy had no idea what had happened, but soon found out. For the next 11 hours it was her job to treat as many people as she could and tell families what she knew—if she knew anything at all--about their loved ones. It was also her job to somehow calm and reassure those terrified relatives.

She told them what she knew. If she knew nothing, she told them that too.

Around this time Tammy's brother Troy Aikman was getting ready to hit a golf ball in a celebrity tournament in Florida. She called him: "Troy, I'm okay, but I need you now more than I've ever needed anyone in my life. Something terrible happened at the Murrah building. They're bringing in dead and dying people and I'm overwhelmed."

From that day on to today, Super Bowl champion and Pro Football Hall of Famer Troy Aikman remains convinced that his sister is the biggest hero in the family. Her anguish and harrowing experience were a shining example of commitment, courage, and determination. It happened 24 years ago, but Troy has never forgotten his sister and what she endured.

"I think the difficult part, or why it's emotional for me, is because my sister witnessed the people who were coming in off the streets and they were rushing in. And they didn't have enough beds to get these people to."

Aikman also talked about the visit that he and Cowboys teammates made to Oklahoma City to meet with victims and first responders.

"What came of that, it was like what we witnessed on 9/11," he said.

Just a few weeks later I was with Aikman the day he and many of those teammates visited the hundreds of victims, the critically wounded and the dying. One man who had part of a steel girder nearly decapitate him was in a hospital room when Aikman walked in.

"Oh my God, it's Troy Aikman," the man said. "You're my hero."

Aikman was almost angry as he told me the story later: "Here's a man who was dying telling me that I was some sort of hero to him, and I felt not just embarrassed but almost ashamed."

Troy told me the real heroes were first responders and people who'd sprung into action mere seconds after the bomb went off. "I know people have always looked up to athletes, and I get and appreciate their admiration. But my sister and people like her saw things that day that will forever be etched in their memory. Horrible things, and things that time can't erase."

A few months later I went to interview Troy and Tammy in Oklahoma City, as we all did what we could to benefit the families who'd lost loved ones or who saw them severely injured. As we spoke about the horror of what she'd seen, Tammy started to cry. Troy asked her to stop.

"I want people to know what a hero is, and it's certainly not a person like me. It's people like my sister, who...," and then Troy's voice cracked. He couldn't go on.

I interviewed many people that week, including one woman who lost twins in the attack. She told me this, and I'm paraphrasing.

I'm grateful to God that I had my children and they brought me love and joy. But in the midst of this horror I'm also grateful to the men and women who sacrificed so much to bring their healing power and mercy to those who lost almost everything. I'm angry sometimes that God would allow this to happen, but then I remember... God also brought us people (like Tammy Aikman) who gave us strength and reminded us that good people are everywhere... and that they far outweigh the evil in this world.

Tammy Aikman briefly left St. Anthony Hospital in 2000. She was asked back a few years ago and in 2013 became the COO and later CEO. She had been with the hospital for 30 years.

She remains, to this day, Troy Aikman's hero.

My Younger Self

"'The past is never dead. It's not even past."
~ William Faulkner
Requiem for a Nun

Of course, the only way to live is in the present. The now. I mostly can do it, but not always. Sometimes I don't want to live in the present. For me the past is much richer, safer, happier, more familiar. My friends were all still alive, as were my folks. Those were much happier times.

I listened to a ton of music, and those songs are still vivid for the profoundly emotional impact they've all had in my life. I remember how much I loved to see those bands that really blew me away in live performances. And my Beatles were with me pretty much all the way in my childhood and adulthood.

They are like old friends. And even today, when I see or hear them, I am present in their past… and never think about what would happen later. They were my love then… and still are.

I remember the great teams I rooted for. The '72 undefeated Dolphins and 3-time World Champ Orioles, the team I was a batboy for.

I grew up in Miami, which was at the time a kind of suburb of New York. I grew up with a NY sensibility. And though I'm not a New Yorker I get New York sentimentality for sure. I'm an orthodox sentimentalist.

My friends? My friends were funny, original and smart. I live in the past when I feel despair. I realize it's all temporary and that you can't stay there long term. But sometimes it sure feels good.

Sometimes I just look at the digital history of what's out there on the internet. I find myself lost in clips of old TV shows, songs from my youth, highlights of teams I loved. I wish I had a chance to go back—even for a day.

I think I'd know what to do and what to say. I was an awkward kid and always shy with girls, but I'd go back in time and pull my younger self aside and tell ME this. I would hope I would listen.

Life gets better and more fun and more enlightening. But it also gets hard and sad, and sometimes it breaks your heart. But live every day with a purpose. Laugh every day and take chances, too. Crank up the music louder. Ask that girl out you were too scared to ask. Run with a crowd of funny people because they help you live your life better. Don't look at the clock, and try, if you can, not to look at the other guy's "plate". Sometimes he will have much more than you. Sometimes he will have much less. But never live with envy and stay away from hate and small people.

I don't have a ton of regrets in my life, but they are there and I don't share them much. Most have to do with lost loves and words I never spoke and letters I never got around to writing. I don't hate the present. So much is better today in so many areas... but if you knew me and came to my house you'd see a salute to the past in virtually every room. My collections, my art, my jukeboxes, my trains... it's all there, and I love it all.

Billy Joel once wrote an obscure song called "Souvenir":

"...and your mementos will all turn to dust... but that's the price you pay. Cos' every year's a souvenir... that slowly fades away."

Live every day with joy and lots of laughs and love really hard and with all your heart. You don't have to live in the past to enjoy the present. But for me, it really helps.

One Night, in a Chinese Restaurant

I love stories about how celebrities get their "stage" names.

In the early 50s, singer songwriter Bob Cossotto from Harlem and later the Bronx was told by his manager that the name was "too ethnic" and he would need another. Bob wanted to keep his name because he was a proud Italian and because his sister, Nina, wanted to keep the family name alive too. One night while he and his manager were eating in a Chinese restaurant, Bob was overruled. The manager told him to make a name change immediately.

Bob looked out the window and saw the sign, "Mandarin Chinese Food" in neon. The only problem was that the first two letters of "Mandarin" were blown out, so all Bob could read was "darin Chinese Food." And just like that the legendary singer we know as Bobby Darin was born.

By the way, all his life, Bobby's sister Nina was close to him. He adored her and she him. Then one day he found out the truth: Nina was his mother.

The Long Journey

Back when he appeared as a regular on my *Up Close* show on ESPN, Hall of Famer Howie Long used to bring his son to the show. One day I was savagely attacked by the son, who vowed to "take me down" with a football tackle.

I nearly had my ankle broken by the marauding Chris Long.

He was five years old.

He was a big kid even then, and my ankle will never forget him.

It's hard to forget Chris Long anyway, not just because he was a decorated two time Super Bowl champ with some 70 sacks in the league and an imposing collection of tattoos decorating his massive torso. No, Chris Long is unforgettable because he a relentless activist, philanthropist, and advocate for social change.

In 2017 Chris donated his entire season paycheck to fund educational opportunities for disadvantaged youngsters in the three cities in which he'd played: St. Louis, Boston, and Philadelphia. But there's *so much more* to Chris' outreach.

Along with teammate William Hayes he spent time on the streets of St. Louis to learn about what it's like to live as a homeless citizen. It opened his eyes.

He became energized and mobilized to try to make a difference in the world, beginning in this country with literacy and educational programs, fund-raising for America's vets; and in East Africa, where he spearheaded a "Waterboys" program to provide drought-stricken regions in Tanzania some 60 wells, quenching the thirsts of about a quarter of a million people.

"I got this opportunity to make a difference, but it wasn't me alone," Chris explained. "I wanted to build a team of former and current NFL players and our vets to make a difference for people who we would never know."

Long reflected on the virtues of teamwork. "You can't move a mountain on your own, but calling someone and telling them 'you can help' ... galvanizes people. And it's a life-changing experience that will never end for me. In the process of building a team, you change someone else's life in making a difference."

Chris' impact in Africa is still growing, but he's also turned his attention back home to a country divided and seeking a path to unity.

Unlike most white players in the NFL, Long was out front and supportive of the controversial protest of kneeling during the national anthem ... symbolically putting his hand on the shoulder of teammate Malcolm Jenkins in solidarity.

"There's a lot of white players like me who feel the way I do, but they don't have the financial security or personality to join in support of protesting injustice. A lot of players are afraid of it affecting their brand. I happen to think 'branding' people is dumb anyway. Your *brand* should be *you*! And so I am."

Chris talked about the blowback he got on social media.

"I got a lot of hate mail and threats because of my support for Malcolm and Colin Kaepernick. When you get people messaging you that they're going to knock your teeth down your throat with a baseball bat in front of your wife and kids ... well, that pissed me off. It didn't scare me or inhibit me. It *taught* me that we have a real problem in America. It also made me want to find that mother."

Chris added this: "I can only imagine what it's like to be black and to have to deal with this every day. To have lived through the civil rights movement, to *not* say anything would be a sellout.

"I don't like politicians so I have no interest in politics. To me it's a basic issue of right and wrong."

His teammates opened their hearts to Chris and his altruism.

"It was eye-opening to me. It makes you respect Chris that much more," said former teammate Fletcher Cox. "I told him, *this* is what I want to do. To give back to people from where I'm from and for others I'll never know."

From his educational initiatives to his water works programs in Africa to his work with veterans, Long's philosophy remains the same: Bring people together and cause a chain reaction of impact. He's seeking a ripple effect that completely transforms people's lives.

Interestingly, Chris' dad Howie came into the game fueled by insecurity. Howie Long grew up in poverty in Charlestown, Mass. As a child he was passed from family to family. He remembers family members sleeping in cars. Howie developed a deep sense of insecurity and drive based on the fear of losing his livelihood.

Chris Long grew up in affluence. He went to the best schools, wore the best clothes and ate the best food; and yet, it was *his* insecurity that drove him, too.

Ironically, when you have everything I had, this is not a rich kid's game. And while most kids didn't come from having everything, it's also true that most kids didn't have to live up to their dad's legacy as a Hall of Famer either.

So I had to prove myself. I had to work harder. I've always had a chip on my shoulder that comes from everyone having a preconceived notion about me as a player and as a man ... that I'm soft, unmotivated, too comfortable, and probably a prick.

I take everything personally. When you grow up with people telling you it's because of your dad or 'its not your accomplishment,' you get motivated in a hurry or you fail. Even as All-State in Virginia, people thought it was only because of my dad. The truth is, I outworked everybody.

Howie Long is the second of three Howie Longs in his family.

His father was "Howie" too, but the "Hall of Fame Howie" and his son "Howie" aren't "Howie Juniors." That's because the patriarch of the family doesn't necessarily believe in his own legacy, or that others should follow.

He believes in his sons' (Chris, Kyle, and Howie) unique individuality. Their dreams and aspirations should be their own, not his.

I made about $38,000 when I first played for the Raiders. After taxes it was a little more than a thousand dollars a week. And I was sending money home to family members, to people in need. But with no contract guarantees I didn't have the ability to take on social issues and to be outspoken about injustice. I needed to keep my job. But now it's a different time in sports. Chris and Kyle and Howie are doing great things that I could never have dreamed to do when I was a player.

My wife Diane and I are deeply proud of all three boys, and we'd like to think we've been an influence in their social awareness. But the truth is…they are their own people.

Chris was always standing up for people. His brothers, his friends, his teammates. He never cared about money. All he ever cared about was respect. And he believes respect is earned. He's an impressive man. There's no moss on Chris. My whole world since I had kids is 'What can I do for them?' For Chris, it's always been 'What can I do for others?' He's always focusing on the right thing to do. The kind thing to do. The humane thing to do.

I asked Howie to reflect on Chris' legacy, apart from his own.

When history is written of this time in the NFL with social injustice, all of those things, Chris Long's name will be talked about. When I sit back and think about that, I say, 'How remarkable is that?'

What he's done to effectively impact people's lives, in St. Louis, New England, Philadelphia … and Charlottesville … he is a lighthouse in a storm. No matter how big the whitecaps are. No matter how big the waves are. No matter how hard the wind is blowing … he is a rock."

Maybe Chris Long will never be the player his father was, but that's the point. He understands humility and gratitude, and his work off the field made his time in the NFL far more worthy than winning football games.

"I'm not the most talented person in my family or even on the field on any given Sunday. But I made myself a better player and a better man with that chip on my shoulder. Enough is never good enough. That insecurity and pressure served me well, because what I don't have in ability I have in outworking the next guy."

I asked Chris if playing on two world-championship teams gave him enough in life.

"Football is not enough for me. It's not my identity. For some players it's that they became the biggest deal in their hometown or school. Hell, I'm not the biggest deal *in my family!* Football has never made me and will never make me."

There has been criticism of activist athletes that they should somehow keep quiet, play the games, take the paycheck, and be grateful that they have a job. "Stick to sports," they say.

Chris Long doesn't buy it.

I would never tell an accountant to stick to being an accountant. I wouldn't tell the trash man to just collect garbage. I wouldn't tell a doctor to just worry about what goes on in his clinic or hospital. What makes our society great is that everybody has a seat at the table. If I stick to sports, then you have to stick to your job. I think that it doesn't need to be your problem to care about a problem.

In May of 2017, when the Charlottesville white nationalist protest erupted in violence and death, it hit Chris Long even harder than most. Charlottesville is his home. He attended the University of Virginia. The horror literally hit him where he lived.

When it's your hometown it's like 'What are you going to do about it?' That's not just a Charlottesville problem, these people came from out of town, but it is also our problem too. This stuff has been in existence from the beginning of time. But hate is the evil we should all agree to fight.

I put myself in the shoes of people who have to deal with this on a regular basis. For me, it was one weekend in my hometown. For them, the people who are victims of hate ... it's every day. I have to remember that.

Every year for the past four, Chris travels with his wife Megan, friends and teammates to climb Mt. Kilimanjaro in Tanzania.

It's a way to raise awareness and funds for "Waterboys." It's a 20,000 foot climb, but more than that, it's a way for Chris and others to find inspiration.

We've had a blind man summit, and the first female above-the-knee amputee. And every time I see things like that I break down crying. And I didn't cry after we won the first Super Bowl.

A guy named Elliott Ruiz stands out for me. He's a Marine who stepped on a land mine and he's had, like 15 operations. He was supposed to walk with a cane for the rest of his life. He willed himself somehow to climb this mountain. He struggled so badly he got altitude sickness, throwing up every night. Then he made it to the top.

I remember him sitting on a rock, weeping. He said 'I'm not supposed to be here.' I get chills every time I think about it.

In 2019 Chris Long was awarded the Walter Payton NFL Man of the Year Award. I asked Chris to define what it is to be a man.

What defines a man or any person, at least for me, is the impact he (or she) has on the world around them. If you're a solid human being you have a net positive influence on the world around you.

The clock is always ticking. For me, the way I choose to live, I need to squeeze life out of every minute. I lose my mind a bit when I don't have anything to do. But I think, above all, it's about how you love people, how openly you love people, whether it's your teammates, your friends, your kids, your wife, your family. Relationships are really important to me. It's more than achievements.

The Walter Payton Man of the Year award is a great honor, but it's an uncomfortable honor. It implies that I did more, or that I am more deserving than others. This isn't true.

But what I will say is that we've done a great job being productive off the field. If I can give myself even one compliment it's that I'm kind of relentless. I got that from my mom. I would hope that most people would look at our initiatives as creative, and inclusive of other players. It's not a 'me' thing ... it's a 'we' thing. At its most basic, it's about teamwork.

Chris Long may never go to the Hall of Fame like his father, but his spirit is the human embodiment of what truly makes America great.

His passion, caring and commitment represents Americans at their very best.

"America is, after all, still a work in progress."

And so is Chris Long.

A good work in progress.

Mercury Rising

Mercury is an elusive planet. It is also an elusive element. The substance is poisonous if you touch it or get too close.

When I was a kid, Eugene "Mercury" Morris was my favorite football player. Not only because he was an electrifying runner who could score every time he touched the ball, but also because he was elusive, rebellious, outspoken and controversial.

I first met Gene when I was 15. I was a junior counselor at Bob Griese's football camp. I found him fascinating because so many at the time tried to characterize him as a troublemaker. Like Muhammad Ali, Gene was fearless and dared to challenge the status quo. This attracted me. When I got closer I discovered that he wasn't poisonous. This Mercury became even more interesting.

Recently I asked Gene, now 72 years old, why he went against the grain.

I grew up in Pittsburgh, and if you told me not to do something, I'd be the first to do it. Once when I was visiting a friend in Virginia, I went to the movies. They told us that black people had to sit in the balcony. I insisted on the front row. When I was told black people can't date white girls I made sure I dated only white women.

I can best describe it by two films: "To Kill A Mockingbird" and "Roots". The more the establishment tried to deny black people in those movies, the more I knew I wanted to insist on my power, my individuality. They told Kunta Kinte that if he kept running away they would cut off his feet so he could run no more. They said they would cut off his balls if he persisted, so he couldn't father children. I remember saying, 'That'll never be me.'

At West Texas State Merc led the NCAA in many rushing categories. He was second only to O.J. Simpson in total rushing yards. But unlike O.J. as a young man, Gene Morris wasn't a pleaser. He was always someone who pushed convention and authority.

It came from my grandfather, who instilled in me my individuality. I was, deep down, a team player, a born leader. But coaches thought I was too arrogant, too cocky. They missed the point. I wanted the team to win, but I wanted to be the player that led them to win. I remember in college some racist teammates yelled 'the South will rise again!' I walked up to all those white guys and in their face I said, 'Yeah, and I'm gonna lead you to do it.'

Gene Morris played seven years in the NFL. In three of those he made the Pro Bowl. One year he outrushed O.J. Morris became legendary in my hometown of Miami not just for his thrilling play but because he challenged coaches and never backed down.

For many years Morris and Coach Don Shula feuded. But that's long in their rearview mirrors. In fact, Gene Morris and Don Shula have become very close friends, and the great bond of love and friendship between them is deeply moving.

"My grandfather was born on January 6th," said Morris. "I was born on January 5th, Don Shula on January 4th. Those two people on either side of my birthday were probably the most consequential people in my life. In the case of Don it's ironic we were born a day apart because 'likes…repel.'"

That's right. Eugene Morris thinks he is very much like Don Shula. And that's caused friction over the years.

"When I told him [Shula] that he looked up at me and said, 'Oh, so THAT'S it!'"

Morris responded, "Don, that's ALWAYS been it!"

Gene Morris has become a go-to person when Don needs help.

"We made peace with each other," said Morris. "I challenged him as a player and Don didn't like that. I once corrected his pronunciation of a word in a team meeting and he didn't like it. That was 48 years ago in our first year together. He began to sarcastically enunciate my formal name. He'd say 'Okay, Eu-Gene.' That started off the back and forth thing."

He continued.

Don and I were at odds with each other for years. I didn't go to the 10th reunion of the '72 undefeated Dolphins because I was in jail. At the 20th I didn't want to go. Shula and I had this thing going. We were not friendly. I had disdain for him for trading me away to San Diego. Larry Little (Hall of Fame guard) pulled me aside and said, 'Merc, this isn't about you. This isn't about Don. This isn't about your feud. This is about our TEAM. This is for the guys you played with.'

And so I sat down and wrote Don a letter. I said, 'Don, when you traded me to San Diego I said your team would be no better without me. And you know what? After I left, the Dolphins went 6-8. But in San Diego WE went 6-8 too, so we were BOTH no better without each other. I have a lot of respect for you and I know you won't write this letter, so I will.'

And then Don wrote me a note back and said, 'I'm glad you finally came around.'"

Morris laughed hard at that.

His two best years were MY two best years. The point is, we needed each other. He gave me the opportunity, and together WE delivered. And the back and forth thing still continues to this day, but the needle back and forth comes from love and respect.

Likes repel! Two like magnets can't attract.

I've spent time around Shula and Morris together and it's really something to see. They are funny, playful, and even tender. I was

102

making a comment about Don Shula, now 88 years old, having to navigate using a wheelchair and Morris quickly corrected me.

"Roy, Don is NOT in a wheelchair. He uses a scooter. There's a world of difference. And he's as sharp as he's ever been."

It was like Gene Morris was protecting a father, a friend, someone he loves.

Gene Morris turned 72 in January, 2019. He lost a son in a car wreck two years ago. Teammates and friends of his have died. Don Shula hit 89 the day before Morris. He lost his first wife to cancer, and most of his coaching colleagues and many of his favorite players have passed too.

Mortality is creeping up on both. The reality is not lost on either.

In the weeks that followed my conversation with Morris, another teammate, Hall of Famer and captain of the "no-name defense" Nick Buoniconti died, likely because of CTE. Gene was devastated.

"I realize that we needed each other back then. And we won because he gave me the chance, and I made good on my chance. And now as the clock is running out in life we need each other more than ever."

So do we all.

As I mentioned, in June of 2016 Morris lost one of his twin sons, Jarrett, in an early morning car accident. It was Jarrett's birthday. Gene's girlfriend Debbie Ronca awakened him and said, "Gene, I have some very, very sad news. Jarrett was killed in a car accident."

Gene thought she was talking about her own son, also named Jarrett, and went to hug her, and said, "I'm so sorry, Debbie." Then Debbie told Gene that it was HIS son who was killed, not hers.

"I think losing that boy kind of broke Gene," said Ronca. "He didn't talk to people for a long time, and in some ways he's still only slowly accepting it."

Gene told me he still has Jarrett's ashes in a container in his garage. He hasn't yet decided what to do with it.

"I thank God I had told Jarrett on Father's Day that I was proud of him for raising his little girl Molly the right way," Morris said. "It was the last thing I ever said to my boy. My daughter Tiffany will now raise Molly. I'm immensely proud of her for taking on that responsibility."

Losing a child has been one of many painful experiences in Gene's life. In 1982 he was arrested on charges of drug trafficking, and in 1983 sentenced to 20 years in prison with a mandatory fifteen-year term. Morris freely admits to using cocaine but vehemently denies he'd ever tried to traffic the drug. He could have served the full term, but in March of 1986 his conviction was overturned by the Florida Supreme Court. Evidence he had offered to prove entrapment had been excluded as hearsay under a mistaken characterization. He was granted a new trial and reached a plea bargain, resulting in his release from prison May 23, 1986 after having served three years.

One of the greatest heartbreaks of my life was that my parents never lived to see me come out of prison. They allowed me to visit my mother when she was ill. She told me she would be willing to serve the time for me because she was living on borrowed time. I didn't realize what she meant. I didn't know she was terminal. I remember the only way they would give me a supervised pass out of prison was if I apologized for insulting the prosecutor. I wasn't sorry because I knew the truth, but I begrudgingly apologized so I could see my mother. My mom was dead within days of my visit, my father not long after that. For the rest of my life I will fight the state of Florida to clear my name. I want an acknowledgement that they set me up."

To this day Gene Morris has two framed jerseys on his wall. One is the Dolphin jersey awarded for being named one of the 50 greatest Dolphins ever. The other "jersey" is the prison uniform he wore for three years.

"36 years later I decided to frame the two garments that had dramatically impacted my life forever—the number 22 and the number 088586. These two garments with these two numbers are why this entire story even exists for me to tell, let alone share with the public. It is a necessary step in clearing my name, for mom and dad."

Gene Morris has never been one to follow convention. Former teammate wide receiver Nat Moore told him to wear an aqua-colored jacket when the 1972 Dolphins were invited to the White House to be honored by President Obama.

I wasn't going to wear what everyone else would wear. I read that White House protocol said I should wear business attire. I didn't want to look like I was a member of some glee club, so I wore a black suit. When the president shook my hand he said, 'You're the only one wearing the right thing.' We both cracked up."

Gene Morris has always has been a warrior. He fights for pensions and benefits for retired players and insists that the settlement that the league made with pre-1993 players was inadequate. He has personally fought for numerous players who were denied medical coverage.

This is an issue close to Gene's heart because one of his teammates is Jim Kiick, who has been diagnosed with dementia. Kiick now lives in an assisted living facility in Broward County, Florida. Morris frequently drives from his home far to the south near Homestead to visit Kiick, a trip that often takes hours.

"Last night he asked the same question maybe 25 times, and the day before 18 (and I'm not exaggerating). It's always whether I was coming to a fundraiser. I don't get angry or even frustrated. I just calmly pick up the phone and answer the question. I'm here to reassure him."

Morris then starts to weep over the phone.

I see him suffering, man, and I don't see any way out for him. But the little bit that's left, that's still 'him.' THAT'S the part I connect to. It finally got to me and I started weeping because he's my friend and I've been connected to him since he was a young guy. (fullback Larry) Csonka and Kiick were Butch and Sundance. They were on Johnny Carson. They were beloved. And then I took his spot in the starting lineup. It hurt him to lose his job but then he realized it was better for the team. And that's why he knows I'll always be there for him. It's better for the 'team' now too."

Morris adds:

My grandfather died and I didn't go to his funeral because I couldn't deal with the pain and sadness. I still regret that to this day. Some of my teammates on the Dolphins don't want to see Jim Kiick this way, but I'm not going to forsake my responsibility to people I love any more. I'm not going to make that same mistake, to insulate my own sadness, and fear, and pain. I'm there for Jim. And I'll always be there for Jim. So he can call me another 25 times and ask me the exact same thing. It's nothing to me. It's not even inconvenient any more.

I then told Gene that I could sum this up in one word: "Brotherhood."

It is. And you know something? I never thought I'd be the guy to take this kind of thing on, but Jim has a son named Austin who may be afraid or sad or angry that his dad is this way. I told Austin that I saw him become frustrated with his dad in front of other people. I said, 'Austin, your dad is the same as me. If something he says or does pisses you off, remember he's a part of you and you are a part of him. Don't you EVER show embarrassment or anger with your dad in public.'

I've always admired the rebel in Gene Morris. I've always admired the fighter, and the funny guy too. No one is funnier than Merc. But now as I get older and he does too, more than anything else I'm impressed with his heart. I don't know that I've ever met anyone MORE devoted than Gene Morris. In his time he was a player who ran against the grain. And in his time since, Morris has challenged the system and suffered blows—some of them grievous and heartbreaking—but always found a way to bounce back up. As great a player and activist and fighter he is ... to me, he belongs in the Hall of Fame of human beings.

Love After Tennis

The most "giving" athlete I've ever met? The competition's not even close. And it's someone hardly anyone thinks of or even knows about anymore. In 1980 (at the age of 15 years, 19 days), she became the youngest player ever to be seeded at Wimbledon, a record that was broken by Jennifer Capriati in 1990. After defeating former champion Virginia Wade, she became the youngest quarter finalist in the history of the tournament. Later in the year she became the youngest semifinalist in US Open history.

Her name is Andrea Jaeger and she was often compared to John McEnroe because of her screaming and arguing over line calls. She was very talented, but troubled too.

At one point she was the number two ranked woman tennis player in the world. During her career Jaeger won $1.4 million in prize money and millions more in endorsements.

One day while on tour she visited a children's cancer hospital. She was so moved and affected by her visit that in 1990 she used her winnings from tennis to create the Silver Lining Foundation with her close friend and business partner Heidi Bookout. Located in Aspen, Colorado, the organization transported groups of young cancer patients to the resort town for a week of support and activities, including horseback riding and whitewater rafting. The foundation also provided money for reunions, family campouts, college scholarships, medical internships, and other programs for children who could not travel. The organization had other powerful backers, both in the world of sports and elsewhere. The first contributor was John McEnroe. Many high-profile celebrities were also involved, including Andre Agassi, Pete Sampras, and David Robinson.

In 1996 Jaeger received the Samuel S. Beard Award for Greatest Public Service by an Individual 35 Years or Under, an accolade given out annually by Jefferson Awards. This was no one-time thing for Andrea. She gave nearly every penny she ever had to this foundation. She even sold her car to fund it. I was fortunate to have joined Andrea and Monica Seles, another tennis great, for a Silver Lining Foundation fundraiser many years ago. The photo is below.

Andrea found her calling and her soul with this foundation. Her smile in this photo is a smile of deep satisfaction in service. She wrote a book and the title defined her: *First Serve*.

In 2006 she became "Sister Andrea," a member of the Anglican Order of Preachers. She is a member of the Episcopal Church and based in Santa Rosa Beach, Florida.

When I think of athletes who serve, no one has ever served longer and with more commitment than Andrea Jaeger. And tennis ended up having little to do with her "serve."

She is one of the most impressive people I've ever known in sports.

The Hitter with a Heart

I'm changing the subject because I want to, and I have to. I want to tell you about something about life that all of us know. Life can be so exhilarating and joyful and yet, in the same life, there can be so much heartbreak and sadness.

What follows is a story about someone most of you know. This man was the very best at his profession. He achieved so much and yet suffered so much pain, heartbreak and loss. He was born on a train in Panama over 70 years ago. His mother was a domestic, and in the late 1940s in Panama, whites and blacks were separated. His mother went into labor on the train. Only because of the kindness of a Jewish doctor named Rodney Cline was this baby born without complications. Dr. Rodney Cline delivered the baby, and the mother was so grateful she named her son Rodney Cline Carew.

We all know Rod Carew, who with Tony Gwynn was probably the greatest hitter of his generation. He held 7 batting titles, had 3,000 hits, and went to the Hall of Fame. They named the AL batting title award after Rod. Life seemed so effortless for Rod Carew. But life has a tendency to throw a lot of curves. After he retired, Rod faced a battle with gum and jaw cancer.

All his life he had chewed tobacco on the field. The cancer was caught early, and unlike his friend and hitting colleague Tony Gwynn, did not kill him. He lost most of his teeth and part of his jaw, but he survived. It cost him more than $100,000 just to reconstruct his mouth. But he was alive.

Then his daughter Michelle got a rare form of leukemia at a very young age. Suddenly Rod's life turned upside down. The only thing that could save Michelle was a bone marrow transplant, but they couldn't find a match. They tried an experimental treatment and it failed. Michelle died at age 18. Rod and his family were devastated.

I didn't know Rod well as a player because he was standoffish to the media and TV folks like me, but when I volunteered to host his fundraisers for Children's Hospital in Orange County, California, I saw a warmer, accessible, reflective Rod Carew. We became friends and he appreciated everything I had done, and everything everyone else did for him.

Then one day he suffered a massive heart attack on a golf course. He should have died, but paramedics brought him back to life. He got another chance. His heart was so scarred and damaged that he would need a heart transplant *and* a kidney transplant. One day, Konrad Reuland, the Baltimore Ravens' tight end, suffered a brain aneurysm and died. His family knew Rod's family because their kids attended the same school.

Rod was given a new heart and a new kidney by Konrad's mother Mary. Three months later, Rod met her. According to news accounts, Mary Reuland greeted Carew with a big hug and told him, "You're part of our family now."

As of this writing, Rod Carew is 73. He has a new lease on life and lives every day with appreciation and gratitude. His journey has been glorious, shattering, wonderful and soul crushing, but he is *alive.*

Sometimes when you think about all our divisions and our differences, when you believe our borders will destroy us as a people, think of how fragile and tenuous our lives are.

But while you're at it, think also of generosity and kindness and the human capacity to persevere, precisely because our humanity is stronger when we think of one another.

For Rod, throughout his life, good people sustained him. Dr. Rodney Cline, the doctor who delivered him. The doctors who saved him from jaw cancer. The doctors who tried to save Michelle. The paramedics who saved him on that golf course. The football player and his family who donated a heart and kidney so that Rod Carew could live. Don't tell Rod Carew that we can't overcome problems we face.

Maya Angelou put it best:

"We need Joy as we need air. We need Love as we need water. We need each other as we need the earth we share."

Don't ever forget that. Not ever.

111

Not So Tiny Tim

Yep, I love this guy. I don't think he'll make it to the majors any time soon unless it's a purely promotional call-up, but as a human being, he's a Hall of Famer.

Tim Tebow stood in the on-deck circle preparing for an at-bat against the Charlotte Stone Crabs when something caught his eye: A young fan was trying to get his attention. Seth Bosch, nine years old at the time, has high-functioning autism. He also suffers from neurofibromatosis—a genetic disorder that causes tumors to form on nerve tissue. The disease left Seth with a tumor behind his right eye, but he was still determined to make his way from his parents' seats behind home plate at Charlotte Sports Park to the protective backstop netting near the Mets' dugout. He really, really wanted to meet Tebow.

Soon after, the Stone Crabs called for a meeting on the mound. The umpire called time while Seth began waving for Tebow to come over. Tebow was more than happy to oblige—he walked over, said hello, and shook Seth's hand through the netting. And then, as if ripped straight from a Hollywood screenplay, he hit a three-run homer!

The dinger was Tebow's fifth since being called up to the High-A St. Lucie Mets, but it's safe to say that it's the most important one he'd hit all year.

"When Seth came back to his seat, he was crying," lleanna Bosch, Seth's mom, told the *Tampa Bay Times*. And then Tim hit the homer. I started crying, too. How does that happen?"

112

Glen and Jimmy

l had a tough time with the passing of Glen Campbell, truly one of my musical idols, so please indulge me with yet another story. This one's a beaut.

It is from Stephen Betts of *Rolling Stone* magazine, so he deserves credit.

When songwriter Jimmy Webb was just 14 years old he was driving a tractor in Laverne, Oklahoma and listening to a transistor radio. On the radio came a song that Glen sang "Turn Around...Look at Me." So blown away by the song and the voice, Webb drove his tractor into a ditch. He made the decision, that day, that he would someday write a song for Glen Campbell. He prayed night after night for that to happen.

Six years later, Jimmy Webb, who was not yet 21 years old, wrote "By the Time I Get to Phoenix." Glen recorded that song and it began Webb's career as a songwriter. Glen's career took off vocally after

years as a studio guitarist, and one of the very best. The two men were about as different as you could find in friends. Politically different. Culturally different. But they were linked by the music.

Webb would write "Wichita Lineman," "Galveston," "Adios," "Where's the Playground Susie?" and many other songs for Glen. Webb was prolific. He wrote "Up, Up and Away" and "MacArthur Park" among many others, but Glen was his most profound inspiration. Webb told *Rolling Stone* that Campbell belongs in the Rock and Roll Hall of Fame. When Campbell died from Alzheimer's disease, Webb posted a heartfelt remembrance on Facebook, writing in part:

> *Well, that moment has come that we have known was an inevitable certainty and yet stings like a sudden catastrophe. Let the world note that a great American influence on pop music, the American Beatle, the secret link between so many artists and records that we can only marvel, has passed and cannot be replaced. He was bountiful. His was a world of gifts freely exchanged: Roger Miller stories, songs from the best writers, an old Merle Haggard record or a pocket knife.*

In the post Webb touched on Campbell's consummate musicianship, noting his inspiration on the development of the Beach Boys' sound (as a key member of the famed "Wrecking Crew," the group of L.A. studio players who backed countless influential recordings throughout the 60s and 70s) and his love for everything from the Righteous Brothers to Flatt & Scruggs. He also observed that the *raison d'etre* for every Glen Campbell show was to bring every suffering soul within the sound of his voice up a peg or two.

Leave 'em laughin'. Leave them feeling just a little tad better about themselves; even though he might have to make them cry a couple of times to get 'em there. What a majestically graceful and kind, top rate performer was Glen on his worst night!

In an interview earlier this year, Webb told *Rolling Stone Country*,

"I believe that Glen was to American music what the Beatles were to British music. I'm not talking about my songs, I'm talking about the countless records that he played on, including "You've Lost That Lovin' Feeling," "Viva Las Vegas," "Johnny Angel," "Along Comes Mary," records with the Velvet Underground, Jefferson Airplane, and the Mamas and Papas. He played with all kinds of genres, with different instrumentation and different styles. If it was a just and righteous world, Glen would be credited as one of the great seminal influences of all time. He was a secret weapon in the armory of 60s record producers."

Webb mentions in the article that when Campbell received his Alzheimer's diagnosis in 2011, he simply said, "Well, I ain't done yet."

Said Webb: "One in a million people would say that. Most people would be crushed and try to figure out what they're going to do, but he just said, 'I'm not done. I'm gonna play somethin'.' He was really an extraordinary character."

What an extraordinary musical and personal friendship Webb and Campbell had. And it was all because of that transistor radio on a tractor in Laverne, Oklahoma on that day in 1961.

Whew!

Best Friends

They were best friends. They were both musicians and singers and songwriters, so that they were friends is easily explainable. But they had golf as their passion. Nearly weekly when they were in town, they would play golf. They would laugh, and crack each other up, and talk about music, and tell great "war stories" about the music business.

One day one of the friends told a joke. Then he repeated the same joke on every hole. Something was wrong. He kept repeating the same story, and it started worrying his golf buddies. He was showing signs of early dementia and Alzheimer's. The two friends would

play golf and drive to the course all the time, until one day one of the friends could not remember how to get there. He didn't even remember he was playing golf. The other began to worry.

The friends were no longer drinking. Both had been sober after long battles with drugs and alcohol. They decided to get the friend to a doctor: their worst fears were realized.

It was, indeed, Alzheimer's. The golfing buddies saw each other regularly until the disease made it too tough to play, so they would stay home and talk about their faith. Both were "born again" Christians. For parts of 50 years, Glen Campbell and Alice Cooper were the best of friends, until Glen's illness made it impossible for the friendship to thrive in ways it always had before. The friendship and support was there from "Alice" ... but Glen was no longer "Glen." The families were close. The wives were close.

The friendship never ended, until Glen could no longer recognize almost anyone.

Today Alice Cooper misses his best pal Glen. He misses the golf, the laughs, and the friendship. Alzheimer's is such a cruel thief.

The Ones Who Saved the World

They came at dawn in high seas and bad weather. It was the windiest day there in 20 years. As far as the eye could see…they were coming.

They came in Higgins boats—DUKW ("duck") boats. They came on barges and battleships, and on amphibious crafts never before seen in battle. They came on floating tanks, most of which sank to the bottom as the battle began.

They came from the skies as paratroopers and nearly half never returned. The came in the darkest time of the night…and then in early dawn.

Thousands of them never had a chance: The vast majority of the men who died perished in the very first waves of the attack. The first soldiers out of the landing craft were gunned down by German artillery. Once those pillboxes were destroyed and the machine guns silenced, the later waves of troops faced far better odds.

They came in all ages, colors and faiths. White and brown and red. Black and yellow. Christians and Jews, Muslims, Hindus and Buddhists. Atheists too.

They were brave and terrified, resolute and daring…but most were scared out of their minds. They were as young as 17 and one, Theodore Roosevelt the second, the former President's eldest son, was the oldest at 56. He didn't survive.

4,000 ships. 11,000 planes. The biggest amphibious assault in history.

It was a complete surprise. And yet the Nazis were prepared for them. They flooded the fields, they mined the beaches, and they took aim at the soldiers as if they were targets in a shooting gallery. These brave young men held the future of Western civilization in their hands.

Because of bad weather and fierce German resistance the D-Day beach landings were chaotic and bloody, with the first waves of landing forces suffering terrible losses—particularly the U.S. troops at Omaha Beach and the Canadian divisions at Juno Beach. But thanks to raw perseverance and grit, the Allies overcame those grave initial setbacks and took all five Normandy beaches by nightfall.

Today, 75 years later, as we go to work, take our children or grandchildren to school, or spend leisure time, we are free. Because they made the ultimate sacrifice we owe a debt to them we can never repay.

The numbers are staggering. On D-Day the allies landed some 156,000. Nearly half were Americans. That's 23,250 on Utah Beach, 34,250 on Omaha Beach and 15,000 airborne.

The losses were mind-boggling too. Of the 4,414 Allied deaths on June 6th, 2,501 were Americans and 1,913 were other nationalities. All on one day.

The long battles were grizzly and gruesome. Confusion and carnage were everywhere. Dead bodies, bloodied bodies, broken bodies. But they persevered. It was the turning point in the Second World War in Europe. In less than a year, the Nazis were defeated.

At the National D-Day Memorial in Bedford, Virginia there are 4,414 names enshrined in bronze plaques: representing every Allied soldier, sailor, airman and Coast Guardsman who died that day.

Tom Hanks, who starred in *Saving Private Ryan*, the film that most vividly captured the horror and the heroics of D-Day, said of the valor of ordinary people doing something extraordinary…

"I think the danger is that it enters into some sort of mythological place. If we ever forget that it was a bunch of individuals that went over, and they all had names like Ernie, and Buck, and Robert—that's when we've done a bad job of being citizens of the world, I think."

And yet so many of us HAVE forgotten. So many of us have taken so much for granted.

The veterans of the Normandy Invasion and those who fought for America's freedom in World War II are dying at a rate of close to 400 a day.

16 million Americans served in that war. Fewer than 500,000 remain.

So today, as you enjoy the freedom to live in a democracy and bask in those freedoms:

The freedom of the press.

The freedom to worship.

The freedom to criticize and protest your government.

Remember those whose blood and limbs and lives were lost on those beaches. Remember the sacrifice. Cherish not their lust of conquest, but their fight to END the conquest. Their fight to liberate.

These are the champions who freed a continent, and in doing so liberated the planet from tyranny and hate. "The eyes of the world are upon you," said General Eisenhower as those men took to battle.

"Prayers of liberty-loving people everywhere march with you."

Today we hold their memory in our hearts and minds. They did nothing less than save the world. They fought for life itself.

Always remember.

Never, ever forget.

The Dean of Stair Climbing

Dean Smith wanted to kill me.

The legendary North Carolina basketball coach—easily one of the most admired coaches in sports history—had just led his Tarheel team to the 1993 National Championship. (Some might remember the game for Chris Webber's ill-advised timeout, which Michigan didn't have). The game was at the Superdome in New Orleans and he had promised me a "one-on-one" interview if the Tarheels won. The only problem was our camera crew was set up on the sixth floor of the Superdome.

"Hey Coach, congratulations. I'm so happy to have you come on my show," I said as I walked into the press room.

Smith: "Thanks Roy, I'm thrilled too. Where ya at?"

"Uh, Coach, unfortunately we're up on the 6th level."

Smith was also legendary for not wanting to be interviewed, but a promise was a promise. It's now almost midnight in the Superdome. Everyone had left an hour ago.

"Don't worry, Coach, we'll take the elevator, and you'll be there in thirty seconds."

Smith was already reluctant, but I was desperate to have him for the show the next day, and he haltingly obliged.

"Okay, Roy," he said, "where's the elevator?"

"Over here, Coach."

I pressed the elevator button: nothing. The Superdome had shut off the elevators and was beginning to turn off the lights, too.

There were stairs… but by now it's midnight on the same night Smith saw his team win the title, plus he was a big smoker. He had little or no energy to walk even one flight of stairs.

We see a man in a golf cart. Thank God, I thought, we'll get a ride to the sixth floor. But the guy in the golf cart has **no idea** who we are. He asks for our passes, but we'd both taken them off after the game. "No passes, no ride," he says, and he motors off.

So now I have to walk six flights of stairs with the legendary coach, who probably had no interest in doing the interview in the first place. We began to climb. Every step was labored; Smith was wheezing and could barely breathe. "How much farther, Roy?" he asked. I could see he was understandably losing patience as well as his breath. We ascended two more flights and Coach Smith had to sit down.

"Roy, I'm telling you, I'm only doing this because I promised you. But I'm beat."

We went up two more flights. The coach was sweating profusely and was barely able to breathe. I was afraid he was going to have a heart attack. As we continued up I tried to get his mind off the climb.

"Jim Lampley (broadcaster and Tarheel) says 'Hi,'" I offered. Smith wasn't having it.

"How much longer, Roy?"

Finally we reached our crew. They were ready and so was Coach Smith.

"I'm giving you ten minutes, and I'm going to set my stopwatch, starting now," he said.

Smith gave me a great interview about the game in *exactly* ten minutes, and we were done. Almost. Now we had to walk back down. Easier, but not easy for a 63-year-old man who'd kept his promise but wanted to be with his team. It's now 1 a.m. in New Orleans. We go to the bottom of the Dome and the doors to the outside are **locked**!!

Finally we find the same maintenance guy on the cart again and he opens the door for us.

"Don't you fellas never come in here again without a pass," he said.

Dean Smith had to hail a cab to get back to the hotel to be with his National Championship team.

In all my years of doing interviews, that was the hardest and most humiliating personally. But Dean Smith kept his word. Years later I saw the coach at a fundraiser I was hosting for the USOC.

"Hey Roy," he said. "No interviews tonight, okay? Besides, we don't have a pass."

The Nicest Neighborhood

My broadcast hero was Fred Rogers. Everything about him was sincere and authentic.

For 33 years, on *Mr. Rogers' Neighborhood*, he gently offered examples of beauty, and wonder, and love, and acceptance, and he did it without judgment and cynicism. When he accepted the honor as a member of the television Hall of Fame in 1999, Fred Rogers stood at the podium and offered these words:

Fame is a four letter word. And like 'tape' or 'zoom' or 'face' or 'pain' or 'life' or 'love,' what ultimately matters is what we do with it. I feel that those of us in television are chosen to be servants. It doesn't matter our particular job, we are chosen to help meet the deeper needs of those who watch and listen to us day and night.

The conductor of the Hollywood Bowl grew up in a family that had little interest in music but he often tells people he found his early inspiration from the fine musicians on television.

Last month, a 13-year-old boy abducted an 8-year-old girl. And when people asked him "why", he said he learned about it on TV. "Something different to try," he said. "Life is cheap ... what does it matter?"

*Well, life isn't cheap. It's the greatest mystery of any millennium. And television needs to do all it can to broadcast that. To show and tell what the good in life is all about. But how do we make goodness ... attractive? By doing whatever we can to bring courage to those whose lives move near our own. By treating our neighbor at least as well as we treat ourselves. And allowing **that** to inform everything that we produce. Who in your life has been such a servant to you? Who has helped you to love the good that grows within you?*

He then asked that every member of the audience take ten seconds of silence to remember those people.

No matter where they are…either here or in heaven…imagine how pleased those people must be to feel you thinking of them now. We only have one life to live on earth. And through television we have the choice of encouraging others to demean this life or to cherish it in creative or imaginative ways.

Fred Rogers has been gone for 15 years now, but his imprint on children, many now adults, is worth remembering and cherishing. We should live the very things he helped so gently teach us. That goodness is more important than greatness. That kindness and love are life's greatest virtues. I loved being a part of Mr. Roger's neighborhood. I hope to live there forever in anything I do.

Are You *Sure* This Isn't North Carolina...?

When Jim Valvano accepted the coaching job at NC State—having never even been to the South—he wanted to do a fundraising pep rally. So the school set up a dinner in Greenville, North Carolina. Jim bought his plane ticket for Greenville ... except it was Greenville, **South Carolina**. He landed, grabbed a cab, and told the driver to take him to the convention center. The cabbie told him, "We don't really have a convention center here... what are you here for?"

Valvano: "I'm the new coach of the Wolfpack"

Cabbie: "We hate all the Wolfpack teams here; in fact we hate all North Carolina teams."

Valvano: "We'll be going to try and change that ..."

Cabbie: "**We'll never change!**"

Valvano said to himself, "Boy, this job is gonna be tougher than I thought."

By the time he figured out he was in the wrong state the pep rally had come and gone. Coach V had missed his first appearance as NC State Coach.

He took the job anyway, and his team went on to win the NCAA title in 1983. A month later he got a letter from that taxi driver.

"Well at least you finally got to the right place," the cabbie wrote. "But we still hate the Wolfpack here in Greenville!"

All Heart: The Singing Policeman

As a boy growing up in Birmingham, Alabama, Francois Clemmons saw that black people were treated differently than whites.

"I could never understand why families left their homes in the early morning hours," he said. "And then I learned about threats from the Klan."

Clemmons grew up with fear and dysfunction everywhere. His parents, who married when they were 15, fought constantly. It wasn't just with words.

They physically beat each other all the time, to such a point that relatives moved me to Youngstown, Ohio. I hoped people in Ohio would treat me better, but even there I was told by my grandmother I couldn't attend the same schools as white people. The only difference between growing up in Alabama and Ohio was that in Ohio, at least they smiled at you when they discriminated against you.

Clemmons found that music soothed his anguish. He sang in different churches.

A social worker paid for my voice lessons. I sang 'Ava Maria.' I sang gospel. I sang Italian opera and Bach. I was comforted by the power and glory of the music. I had the gates of heaven open up when I sang. It was freedom from fear and hate. It calmed me, but it also awakened something in me. When I was 9 or 10, I realized I was gay.

Clemmons kept his homosexuality a secret because he knew the church would condemn him if they knew about it.

I knew what I felt about being gay. You couldn't pray it away, and all the churches where I sang at the time would've rejected me if they knew. I was repressed and miserable. As I got older I hated myself. In my sophomore years at Oberlin College, I seriously considered suicide.

But the music gave him strength, inspiration and hope.

"I sang the Negro spirituals and found depth and power and uplift in that music. One of them still inspires me. It's called, 'There's a Balm in Gilead,' and reads:

To make the wounded whole
There's balm in Gilead, to heal the sin-sick soul.
Sometimes I feel discouraged and think my work's in vain,
but then my Holy spirit revives my soul again.

Thanks to friends at Oberlin, Clemmons overcame his depression.

"They were alert and sensitive to my conflict and self-hate. They knew who I was and what I was."

As he matured and lived more honestly with himself, Francois Clemmons made concessions so he could sing in church. If he repressed his gayness they would allow him to stay.

"I kept the terms that were forced on me. It was a burden, but I never complained."

One night Francois sang in the Presbyterian Church choir outside of Squirrel Hill in Pittsburgh.

I sang with a woman named Joanne Rogers. She was married to a man who was in the seminary to become a minister. His name was Fred Rogers, and he introduced himself to me after a service, telling me, 'Francois, I have never been more touched by a Good Friday service, and your singing deeply affected me.' Rogers had created a television show for children on WQED in Pittsburgh called Mr. Rogers' Neighborhood, and asked me if I'd be interested in becoming a character. I was intrigued and accepted his offer. The character was a policeman named Officer Clemmons, which was bittersweet for me because I always distrusted policemen growing up in the racist South and segregated Ohio.

I hated cops, but Fred said Officer Clemmons would be a singing policeman. Of course I would be one of the very first African American characters on a children's program. I did four shows in the first year. I felt an obligation to do right for Mr. Rogers. I wasn't raised with good parenting. I wasn't accustomed to anyone's kindness, much less any white man's. I saw in Fred his wisdom, his care. Fred Rogers did things for me that no one ever had. Still, I kept him at a distance because I didn't know what would happen if he ever knew I was gay. There were men who made sexual advances toward me in other churches, so I lived in fear and some hesitation towards Fred. I didn't want him to know my secret and my fear.

One day Clemmons' greatest fear was realized: He was seen at a gay club in Pittsburgh, and word got back to Rogers.

It's funny. Over the years people thought Fred was gay. He wasn't of course. But he was a soft, gentle man in voice and manner, and yet he was strong. He asked me if it were true that I was gay and I said yes. Fred never judged, but he was concerned that if I came out, sponsors might bail. 'Francois, you can stay on the show but I can't allow you to acknowledge your homosexuality or wear an earring or anything like that. I have no issue with your personal life, but I worry that we could lose the show over something like this.'

Clemmons understood. Besides, he was used to repressing his gayness and was even encouraged to marry by friends and family. He did marry for a brief period but the marriage didn't last. He was living a lie.

"I wasn't living an authentic life, but I wasn't angry with Fred. He was still my friend and mentor. In fact I felt that if society was more like Fred Rogers, the country wouldn't have a problem with gay people."

In April of 1968, Martin Luther King Jr was shot and killed by an assassin in Memphis. There were riots in all major US cities, including Pittsburgh.

You could hear the gunshots and see the fires everywhere. I was living in an area that was vulnerable to destruction and violence. Fred called and told me to pack my bags. He got in his car and drove forty minutes to my neighborhood. He brought me back to his home. I stayed with Fred and Joanne Rogers for weeks. It was a time of reckoning.

Less than two months later Bobby Kennedy was killed, and Fred Rogers was deeply troubled.

"He was brokenhearted and I was angry. I was distraught that every time someone stood up for justice and humanity, they were shot dead," said Clemmons.

Rogers had an idea. He would welcome Officer Clemmons into the "neighborhood" and the two of them would chat while they bathed their feet in a children's pool.

It was a symbolic gesture of course, but it was a powerful one for its time. Fred said, 'It's important for all people, especially children, to see we are friends. That it's normal, natural and easy.' And then at the end of the segment Fred made a spiritual gesture. In the Bible it says that Jesus' disciple Peter thought Jesus was too good to wash his feet. Fred didn't wash my feet, but he dried them. It was all symbolic and very subtle. So there I was, a black

man, and Fred, the icon ... dried my feet.

Francois and Fred sang a song together called "There Are Many Ways to Say I Love You." Some of the lyrics go like this:

"There are many ways to say I love you.
There are many ways to say I care about you.
You'll find many ways to understand what love is.
Many ways, many ways…many ways to say…I love you."

What many people don't know is that Mr. Rogers and Officer Clemmons filmed two scenes with their feet in the water: one after the violence of the '60s, and the other in 1993, on Francois Clemmons' last appearance on the *Neighborhood*.

During those twenty or so years between identical scenes, I grew up. The boy who did it the first time didn't understand the ramifications. Fred became something of my guru. He was talking to me all the time during those years. He saw me as his protégé. He told me that I was anointed with a gift, that I would continue to grow in my knowledge of God."

In these deeply disturbing times—and specifically because of where the show was filmed near Squirrel Hill, the site of the October 2018 mass murder at Pittsburgh's Tree of Life synagogue—I wanted Francois to reflect on Fred Rogers' famous quote: "Love is at the root of everything…all learning, all relationships, love…or the lack of it."

He paused for a minute and cleared his throat.

I wear a cloak of gratitude for Fred Rogers. That's what I call it. He was like a vessel for me in expressing who I am, who I became as a human being.

On that final day when he said to the camera, 'I like you just the way you are, you make every day a special day just by being you,' for the first time in my 25 years on the show something in my soul caught fire. I felt it in my chest. When the segment ended I walked over to him and said, 'Fred, were you talking to ME?' He looked me in the eye and said, 'Yes. I have been talking to you for years … but you heard me TODAY.'

My life changed on the spot. I fell into his arms and started crying. I saw Fred Rogers as energy, as love. I didn't see him as a white man. I saw, pure, PURE, unadulterated love. It was so beautiful. He said to me, 'I am here for you, Francois. I will never let you down.' I didn't see him AS God, but I did see him as someone who reflected the love of God.

"Fred Rogers wasn't perfect," said Clemmons, "but he sure as hell was the most perfect human being I ever met."

Brother Ray

The word "genius" is thrown around a lot in the media. Einstein was a genius. Bill Parcells and Bill Belichick and Earl Weaver were not. Stephen Hawking had an IQ of about 160, and was a verifiable genius. But musically speaking, in my lifetime there's only one "genius." It wasn't Elvis, or Paul McCartney or John Lennon, or Jimi Hendrix.

If it weren't for a genius named Ray Robinson (not the fighter), none of those people would've been inspired to be who they became.

Ray Robinson, of course, is Ray Charles.

His musical styles, virtuosity, sounds, ideas, and playing made

him the greatest single pop musical influence in the last half of the 20th century and beyond. Ray was blind from the age of seven, and lived in abject poverty in his early childhood to such a point that he went hungry for days. His first payday was four dollars a night. He thought it felt like a million bucks. His mother was herself an orphan, and she gave birth to Ray when she was 14 years old. The litany of tragedy and setbacks he endured would have leveled almost any other human being. Not Ray.

I won't list his musical accomplishments. They've been well chronicled. He's influenced everyone from Little Richard, the Beatles and the Rolling Stones to Elton John, Billy Joel, and literally thousands of great artists in between. Charles was also an inspiration to Pink Floyd member Roger Waters, who put it this way: "I was about 15. In the middle of the night with friends, we were listening to jazz. It was 'Georgia on My Mind.' Ray Charles's version. Then I thought, 'One day, if I make some people feel only one-twentieth of what I am feeling now, it will be quite enough for me.'"

"Georgia on my Mind" and "I Can't Stop Loving You" are two of my favorite Ray Charles performances on record (*Modern Sounds in Country Music* was a breakthrough record), but they are tied with about a hundred others too.

I will tell you a story about my only interview with "Brother Ray." I'd always wanted to meet him, and I found out that he had an office (in a way) near Western Avenue in Los Angeles, which, at the time, was pretty old and decrepit. Yet there he'd sat at a piano nearly every day for 50 years until he got sick. Almost every in-depth interview was conducted there. He was a sports fan so he knew who I was, but I was shocked that he did.

First, Ray was a champion chess player (you figure that out) and routinely beat his closest friend in life ... Willie Nelson. He knew boxing and, of course, was kidded by Walker Smith (who took the name Ray Robinson and became "Sugar Ray Robinson"). Ray Charles told Sugar Ray that he was the "real Sugar Ray Robinson." By the way, "Sugar" Ray Leonard was named after Ray Charles. His real name is Ray Charles Leonard.

Anyway, Ray knew I had a penchant for wearing colorful suits and he teased me about it.

"Roy, man, sometimes I'm glad I can't see ... like when you wear those suits."

That cracked me up. I asked him if he had any regrets.

He said, "I think I could've been nicer to drummers."

We talked for about an hour about life and loves (Ray Charles has 12 children by 10 different women, though he was only married twice). Then I asked him this question, and it was simple.

"After all you have been through and achieved in life, what has been the hardest lesson to learn?"

Ray didn't hesitate and I'll never forget his answer.

"The hardest thing in life is to know and accept that someone is born to take your place!"

Ray Charles was many things. Most of his life he lived in darkness. But he didn't live in despair. He endured drug addiction, and heartbreak. The loss of his mother and brother devastated him as a child. But he was a bonafide genius in his world, and no one, not pop stars, not hip-hop artists, not jazz artists, could touch him artistically.

I'll never forget the short time I spent with the true genius of music. But he was wrong.

Nobody has been born to "take his place."

Hail To Number 12

Tom Brady has always been accessible for an interview with me. That's always seemed like the good news and still mostly is. But the bad news is, he rarely gives you "anything."

He's got the Derek Jeter thing. Smiles, nervous laughter, and almost never says anything that would make headlines. He never talks about his personal life. He rarely tells you about his preferences—food, drink, politics? Forget it.

All he does is compete and play the game better than anyone ever. Hey, not every QB is Joe Namath, who incidentally wore #12 and is as nice a person as you'd ever want to meet. But Joe gives you unvarnished opinions, truth, and stories. Brady is a shy person and mostly keeps his inner circle very private. If I had to rate the most voluble Superbowl QB it would first be Joe Namath, then Terry Bradshaw (a laugh a minute), then Kenny Stabler (he was football's Jimmy Buffett), and then Roger Staubach, followed by Jim Kelly.

Wanna know what's weird?

All of them wore #12.

That's one list of Superbowl QB greats Brady would never make.

Remembering the King

I have great respect and admiration for LeBron James and I've done a 180 on that.

I didn't like how he handled the Miami "South Beach" thing, but that's long in the past.

LeBron is a great man who gives tens of millions of dollars to his community, stays out of trouble, and practices what he preaches in terms of remembering his very, very, humble roots in Akron. The NBA played 11 games on MLK day today, and when reporters asked him about what Dr. King meant to him, LeBron didn't hold back. He said that what Dr. King stood for, and died for, was about equal opportunities for all, regardless of skin color, faith, gender, or sexual orientation. Then he went further:

"These days in America, racists think it's okay to be out and outspoken without fear. And that's dangerous for us, because it's with you, and it's around every day, but the political and social climate has allowed people to just come out and feel confident about doing negative things."

James also said that citizens have a duty to make things better.

"We all have to continue to come together and shine a brighter light on—I don't want to use the word stupidity, but that's basically what it comes down to. We can't allow that to stop us from continuing to be together and preach the right word of living and loving and laughing and things of that nature. Because would we want to live anywhere else? I don't think so. We love this place."

Amen LeBron.

Kareem Abdul-Jabbar says James is the best example of an athlete with a sense of social justice in the NBA today. LeBron James is carrying a torch for the underprivileged and disenfranchised. I can't think of a better person playing pro sports today.

On this solemn day of respect and acknowledgement of the birth, almost 90 years ago, of the greatest civil rights leader in history, Dr. Martin Luther King Jr., I'd like to share this inspiring story.

When he was just 14 years old, this very tall but gawky and awkward teenager was told he could go listen to a press conference with Dr. King in Harlem, NY. This youngster had heard about Dr. King and was already inspired by the civil rights struggle. He was allowed into the press conference, but there were no chairs left and most people couldn't see over the massive crowd at the microphone.

It didn't matter. He didn't need a chair. He was almost 7 feet tall at age 14 and easily towered over the crowd for great view of Dr. King and his speech. He listened intently and was so moved and inspired he decided, then and there, to make his own dedicated effort in the fight for civil rights. The 14-year-old boy would actually grow taller, and less awkward, and more confident as an athlete. Dr. King knew that this youngster was a "warrior" for civil rights and admired the kid from afar. That kid was Lew Alcindor, who later changed his name and faith. He became Kareem Abdul-Jabbar. Kareem has written 14 books (three this year), mostly about what civil rights in one way or another has meant to him.

Kareem told me this, this weekend:

"Every day, in one way or another, I live my life inspired by Dr. King and what he represented. I want to make my life matter, maybe not in the way Dr. King's did, but I want mine to impact the lives of others, like Dr. King, Jackie Robinson, and others. That speech, that day, from Dr. King, and the fact that I was there, made all the difference in my life's path."

Woah ... Nellie!

Keith Jackson, the legendary broadcaster, died in 2018 at age 89. First of all: an admission.

Keith Jackson *never* said, "Whoa Nellie," on a broadcast. It was another announcer at another time. The "Whoa Nellie" came from me. I was always impersonating Keith and used the "Whoa Nellie" phrase, and for the rest of his career Keith Jackson was saddled with a phrase he'd never uttered. But make no mistake: Keith Jackson was the voice of college football.

And the voice of so many other sports and games. He was "crackling Saturday afternoons," and "big mean uglies ... comin' through the tunnel." He was "soph-A mores" and "yunguns" and a thousand other terms and phrases. He was Saturday afternoons, but he was also the first voice of Monday Night Football and Monday Night Baseball on ABC. He was a self-assured, macho, country spun broadcaster

with a ton of experiences and spins of yarn.

He called stock car racing, "Buddy Baker coming 'round the stretch with Chris E-con-a-mackey on the infield." He called hydrofoil races on the water, drag races, and those crazy dirt and mud wreck races, and every important track and field race in the Olympics. And he called hundreds of golf tournaments, and every one of those broadcasts was called impeccably, appropriately, and with style and panache.

He was the first NBA announcer on ABC TV with Bill Russell, but he also called prizefights, horse races, swimming competitions, diving, and maybe a hundred more events.

I loved Keith.

He was a friend of mine. But he never got too close to people because there was only one real person whom he loved dearly ... his wife of 60 years, Turi Ann. They were inseparable. Only sports ever kept them apart, and really not even then.

Keith was the person who called the Rose Bowl "The Granddaddy of them all." But he did cry "Fuuuuuuuuumble" during his game announcing and *that* was his signature. But Keith was hardly just a lampoonable cartoon. His broadcasts were regal and majestic, and full of grace and gravity.

He dealt with Cosell and Reggie Jackson in the booth, but he was the voice of the game. A few years ago Keith and I spoke at the LA Sportscasters luncheon, and he asked me to impersonate him, and told me to say, "Whoa Nellie," as he would sound.

I was nervous. I didn't want to offend him or disgrace him in any way. I had too much admiration and respect for him to make light of him in his presence. So with trepidation I did the impersonation, and he busted up laughing and told the crowd this great compliment.

"In all the years Roy said I said, 'Whoa Nellie,' I never did. But if I had I'd like it to sound like Roy Firestone said it."

Then he gave me a big Keith Jackson hug. It meant a lot. In all the years I'd "played" him, there was really only one Keith Jackson. He was the genuine article.

Miss you, Keith. You were the very best. There were only imitators (me), but no duplicators.

"Whoa Nellie."

Brad

I've done a million appearances with this guy and I believe, maybe second only to Charles Barkley, that he is the funniest and most spontaneous person I've ever interviewed.

Terry Bradshaw once was in the conversation for the greatest QB of all time, but he was always regarded as "light" in the brain. Not true. He's no Rhodes Scholar, but it takes a quick mind to jump on any subject with wit, irreverence, and even some countrified insight. I love the guy. His personal life has been a mess for years. He's been married at least four times and makes some bad personal choices, but "Brad" is the life of the party and someone you'd love to have as a friend to cheer you up. He's like a real life character from some Dan Jenkins novel.

Not long ago he played himself in a movie called *Father Figures* and did a stint on *Modern Family*. More recently he's appeared on *The Masked Singer*.

Once, behind the curtain in Las Vegas, Terry was in a panic. He told me he didn't know the name of the client he was speaking to or what they did in their industry. Just seconds before he was to appear in front of 2,000 people, I pulled him aside and gave him the name of the company and three or four things to say to make them feel good. For the next 90 minutes Bradshaw not only referenced that name, but also told anecdotes and made observations about their industry (which was door construction for homes). It was an awesome thing to watch.

I believe Terry is a born performer and would've been a wonderful preacher or car salesman. He is that engaging. One of my all time favorite people. He has that "Magic Johnson quality" of making everybody in the room feel he's talking just to them.

Great guy.

One Night in Encino

I never tell Elvis stories because A) I never had any, that is, certainly no *personal* experiences with him, and B) because I liked Elvis as a performer, but I never loved him like I loved the "Fab Four." But here's one story that is a classic that comes from an old friend.

My friend Alan (no last names) was one of the most successful TV producers and show runners during the 60s. He was an executive on the NBC Elvis special and wrote comedy and banter for the King. Elvis was notoriously sweet and unaffected in those years before drugs took hold of him. Anyway, one day Alan and Elvis had a very rare disagreement over a script line. Very uncharacteristically, Elvis got mad at Alan and argued loudly before walking off the set (which was very, very rare for Elvis, almost unprecedented). Alan went back to work on the rest of the show. Later that night, the phone rang at Alan's house. It was Elvis.

"Alan," he said, "I was a real jerk today and I was out of line and I want to apologize."

Alan was surprised and told him there was no need to apologize. Elvis didn't stop there.

"I'd like to make it up to you, Alan, and the only way I know is to perform for you and your friends."

"What do you mean, Elvis?" Alan asked.

Elvis told Alan he wanted to come over to Alan's house *that night* and, as a gift, would perform for Alan's neighbors.

Alan was blown away. Elvis continued.

"Alan, it's 10 o'clock now. I have your home address in Encino. Tell your friends all to come over. I'll be there at 11."

In a driving rain Elvis Presley got on his *motorcycle*, with his guitar, and headed over to Encino.

Alan wasn't sure if this was a put-on or not, but he called five nearby families and friends and told them, "Come to my house at 11 tonight for the surprise of your life."

At 10:45 about 12 people arrived at Alan's house, many in bathrobes and pajamas. They thought Alan was sick or drunk because he wouldn't tell them why he wanted them all there. At 11 the doorbell rang: and there in the flesh was **Elvis Presley**, dripping wet, with his guitar.

Everyone was stunned. Their jaws hit the floor. And for the next 30 minutes Elvis Presley sang and played, told some stories, posed for pictures and signed autographs for everybody. He left around midnight.

The friends left in a haze wondering if they'd seen some sort of hallucination. It was no hallucination. It happened. The next day Elvis was back at work on NBC delivering every line perfectly. The show was a massive hit.

As I said, I wasn't a gigantic Elvis fan. But years later when Alan told me that story, I became one. There was a reason he was called "The King." He was one of the nicest superstars in show business history.

Courage At Six Feet Eleven

Full disclosure: I love Bill Walton.

I loved him as a player. I love him even more as an ex-player. I love him as a friend, an inspiration, and just someone who loves life.

I've met thousands of famous and accomplished people in my life and career, and I can safely say that no one comes even remotely close to William Theodore Walton.

Bill is someone who lives his life at warp speed. Every molecule of his being is dedicated to becoming better, wiser, more enlight-

ened, and more expressive.

His interests are vast. He cherishes deeply. And he articulates all he feels with intense fervor. Many look at him as some sort of cartoon character. Most can't relate to him because they can't keep up with his passions or his drive.

And then there are those who choose to marginalize him as a goofy, free-spirited old hippie who rambles, overexpressing and overstating almost anything and everything. They just don't get it—or him.

Bill credits me with giving him "life," because when no one wanted to use him on television and he appeared as a regular on my original ESPN talk show, *Up Close*, he shined. He developed a following.

It wasn't me giving him a chance. It was Bill Walton making the best of an opportunity.

He found his voice.

I did NOT give him a life.

Bill Walton gave himself his life—and even saved his own life. But more about that later.

Bill squeezes every ounce out of every day until it's wrung out. Life *pours* out of Bill with every fiber of his being, and always has. Basketball was a vehicle for his journey. The game defined Bill, metaphorically and literally.

"I loved basketball from the beginning because of my first coach, Rocky. I loved the nature of the game—the speed, the strategy, the execution, the repetition, the running, the jumping, and the sweating. And I really loved the results."

Bill's "results" were pretty much incomparable. High school phenomenon. All-American. Academic All-American. Three time College Player of the Year. Two National Championships at UCLA with an 88-game winning streak. The number one draft pick in the NBA. Then professionally—two-time NBA champion, and voted one of the 50 greatest players in NBA history.

And yet Bill has lived his life with much regret. Regret for things he feels he didn't accomplish—and for the things he didn't do. A failure to achieve more, to maximize every opportunity.

He uses the words "sorry" and "please" a lot.

I feel in many ways that Bill focuses not on the exhilarating victories, but instead obsesses on what he deems defeat—a torment he imposes on himself about why he didn't do more.

"The 88-game win streak should have been 105. I missed the equivalent of nine and a half of my 14 seasons to injury. That I let down so many people because of injuries no one could see caused me incredible pain and despair that was almost as overwhelming as the pain itself."

Bill was likely the most injured athlete in the history of sports, with 37 orthopedic surgeries stemming from structural and congenital defects in both feet.

"Cursed with my bad feet and lifelong speech impediment, I grew up thinking everyone's feet hurt all the time, and only the lucky ones could talk."

Bill had his first knee surgery when he was just 14. He suffered a broken back while playing at UCLA and never complained because he felt an obligation to his team and to his ability. His body didn't just rebel against him; it revolted and overthrew him.

His injuries left his feet and legs and spine battered and broken. The pain he suffered was almost indescribable.

Bill put it this way:

"The nerve pain in my spine just radiated through my body. It's not like an electric switch where you can turn it on and off. You can't take a pill and the pain goes away. Not for me anyway. It never stopped. You can't sleep; you can't eat. You see no way out. You see no future. The pain I'm describing is worse than anything you could imagine. Imagine being submerged in a vat of scalding acid with an electric current running constantly through it…a burning, stinging, pulsating pain that you can never escape. Ever."

And so Bill suffered in silence—and in conflict.

He quotes one of his favorite literary heroes, George Bernard Shaw: "Be a force of nature instead of a feverish, selfish, little clod of ailments and grievances, complaining that the world will not devote itself to making you happy."

But then the denial peeled away, and the pain took control and he could no longer live the life he sought.

"Seventy-three days on morphine and it does no good. Your spirit is broken," he told me. "My life is over. I can do nothing. I eat my meals stretched out prone on the floor. I have to crawl like a snake to climb up the toilet. I don't think I'm going to make it."

Bill continued.

"My wife Lori, the most beautiful and wonderful of angels, as fine as anything is fine, comes to me. As she gets ever closer, it is just too much, and I cry out in whimpering pain, STOP. Don't come any closer. It's just too much. STOP."

So he thought about suicide.

When you're not in that space, it's inconceivable to take your life. But when you're in that space. When it's you ... it's very clear what your path forward is. Because there IS no path forward and you have to get out from where you are. And the only way that you see at that time ... is to kill yourself. Because death will stop the pain. I won't have any more pain. I told my wife Lori that it was over for me. And that she should go. Get out now, while the going was still good.

But Lori didn't listen. She stayed.

Bill says spinal surgery at UC San Diego Health started his road to recovery. Sportscaster Jim Gray found him the surgeon. Dr. Steven Garfin offered him an innovative surgery option. Bill agreed, but skeptically, as he had seen scores of his surgeries end in failure.

As I was lying on the gurney Dr. Garfin called for the drip to begin, the sedation that would put me to sleep. I'd had that drip far too many times. I knew I didn't have much time left. With my last bit of anything...life, breath, strength, whatever, I begged him as the anesthesia was taking me away. "Please fix me. Please give me one more chance. Please let me play the game of life one more time. Please let me climb the mountain again. Please let me ride my bike one more day.

The surgery took eight and a half hours. There were four incisions. Bill's spine was being reconstructed, and he remained in the hospital for a week.

When he came home Lori would stick Post-it notes on the bed recounting his achievements.

"Today you turned over in bed by yourself."

"Today you were able to sit up at the edge of the bed."

"Today you fed yourself."

"Today you went from your wheelchair to your walker."

March 10, 2009: Bill will never forget that exact date.

He recites the day quickly and with memories of anguish. ESPN suddenly fired him, and with his dismissal he lost his health care coverage.

"It made a horrible situation worse," said Walton. "It was heartbreaking and frightening at the same time. I felt betrayed and terrified that I would not be able to pay for all the years ahead of rehabilitation and care, but that was their decision, and I had to deal with it."

Nine months and hundreds of hours of physical therapy later his spine slowly began to mend. Bill Walton was getting his life back again. Three long years after that ESPN re-hired him. One executive begged to come to his house to make the offer.

"I didn't want them in my house, but they asked me to hear them out. I dropped the bitterness and feeling of resentment toward them. I decided to accept the job again, and it was great to be working and healthy again. Bitterness isn't part of my life anymore."

I asked Bill to reflect on life and what he'd learned during his ordeal.

"I know I would not have made it without other people's help. I know that. But I also know what medicine works—participation in sports, the pool, the weight room, my bike. Being with the other guys on the team who chase their dreams too. But mostly, listening to the music play."

He continued.

"I was so sick and sad, I forgot to turn the music on. I took a big black felt pen and I wrote on a legal pad, 'Turn the music on!' You forget in your hopelessness that there's always something you can do for yourself."

Then I asked Bill what he would have missed had he taken his life.

What I would have missed is the best part of my life. My life today is better than it's ever been. I've spent half my adult life in hospitals. I've spent all of my adult life in chronic pain. Today I am out of pain. I haven't played basketball for 33 years, haven't walked or hiked for pleasure in almost 40. But now I can ride my bike. I can swim. You realize that the worst things that ever happened to you … are really the best things. Because of who you become. Mainly I am happy in love. The surgeries, the medicine … helped me heal eventually … but truly, love carried me through.

Bill reminisced about a legendary influence in his life.

"You know, in his last public comments before he passed, John Wooden, my coach, said he made a mistake by leaving love out of his 'Pyramid of Success.' With everything else going on, I didn't believe it. I didn't understand it. Today I do."

I asked what he has learned most about life itself.

That it's not a straight line to where I am today. It's a long, winding, twisty, rollercoaster ride. And I will never take it for granted. I had my spine fused. I had my ankles fused. There wasn't much they could do for my feet, but I wasn't in pain. I thought it was the end. But it was just a new beginning.

What a marvel Bill Walton is to listen to now. He's ridden his bicycle for 700 miles in California and more than a thousand in Oregon. He talks to spinal patients daily, some in the same plight he once was. He reaches many, although he's seen a few surrender because they couldn't take the pain any longer.

Bill feels the burden of losing those people but is sustained by many who make it through.

"I used to cry for myself, but now I cry with tears of joy when I see others make it to the other side like I did."

I asked him about the person he is today.

"I'm on Bill Walton 19.0 now. I'm the luckiest guy in the world. My life is better because of all the failures. The collapses. The mistakes."

With that in mind I asked him his definition of life.

The driving emotions in my life were hope, opportunity, and purpose. That's what drove me to basketball. But what I have now…is pride, loyalty, and gratitude. Pride is the satisfaction with your choices. Loyalty to doing what it takes to get better. And gratitude is for the people who gave me all of those opportunities. And life … is a celebration of all of those things.

A Stand-Up Guy

I don't consider myself a stand-up comedian at all, though for many years I "worked out" my miserable material at the Improv in Hollywood.

My friend Carrie Snow, who was and is an excellent stand-up, remembers my fledgling attempts that were fueled by sheer gall and nerve (I had some talent, just not enough).

For months and even years, I would "follow" after people like Jerry Seinfeld, Richard Lewis, Jay Leno, Arsenio Hall, Paul Reiser—all "murderers' row" top-notch comedic talent—and occasionally I'd have a halfway decent set.

One night I even followed Eddie Murphy and had my best set ever on the Improv stage.

But I wasn't good at all, not in those people's league anyway.

Richard Lewis who was, and remains, a good friend, told me to watch a comedian friend of his one night after my set. It was 1 am. The guy walked up on the stage and had *absolutely* no command of material, no stage presence and was, in fact, *hostile* to the crowd, and it was no act. He threatened to fight members of his audience. He cursed them, and on a later night had to be restrained physically from going after a heckler. It was an ugly scene, and owner Budd Friedman wanted him barred from the club.

He was, by far, the worst stand-up comedian I had ever heard. Richard asked me what I thought. I only said one word: "awful." Richard told me his friend was really funny but just wasn't cut out for stand-up. Today Richard works on that failed stand-up comedian's show. His name? Larry David.

No Thanks, I've Eaten

I always thought Nolan Ryan's strikeout record of 5,714 is one that will never be broken. *Not ever!*

Imagine. That's nearly 1,000 more career K's than Randy Johnson (who holds second place). It's 20 years of more than 250 strikeouts per year. In the best season of the last few—2016—only three pitchers in all of baseball had 250 or more strikeouts.

Anyway, here's an amazing story that involves Nolan and yours truly.

In the 1990s Nolan called me up and asked me to entertain at the opening of his museum in Alvin, Texas. It's a great showcase with a "Hall of K's" where you can see every strikeout "The Express" had. Claudell Washington, for example, struck out an amazing 48 times in his career against Ryan.

Of course I said "yes" and Nolan gave me a tour of both the museum and his cattle ranch. It was a thrill, because I'm a big Nolan Ryan fan. Ryan is an excellent cattleman and calls it his first real love ... even ahead of baseball.

It was the night of the fundraising dinner and I'm sitting at the table with Nolan and his beautiful wife Ruth. He elbows me and says, "Hey Roy, aren't you gonna have a piece of Henrietta?" I didn't know what he was talking about. He pointed at my plate: there was a massive slab of beef that looked like something out of *The Flintstones*.

"Henrietta," he says. "We milked her for years until she was ready for slaughter."

I was numb.

Nolan Ryan was eating someone he knew. And now he wanted me to take a bite of his friend.

Not only does it freak me out (I haven't eaten beef in 40 years and *never* waver), but I couldn't dare confess this to Nolan Ryan ... especially with a prized cow like Henrietta.

I find a way to get around it though: "Nolan, wow, that's a nice piece of Henrietta there, but I never eat a heavy meal before a performance."

I pick at my salad.

I perform the show.

Everyone is happy.

After the show Nolan comes up to me with a massive, greasy, and bloody bag.

"Thanks for coming, Roy. Now you can go back to the hotel and enjoy Henrietta."

I take the bag, return to my room and summarily drop it in the trash can.

I felt bad, but I didn't want a piece of Henrietta.

I'm still glad I don't eat beef, but I didn't want to have a beef with Nolan Ryan.

If he reads this ... it's a confession.

I hope he understands.

I Can't Hear You!

I like researching and writing about obscure supporting actors in shows I got a kick out of in the 60's. It is always fascinating to learn about unforgettable performers who made the difference in a TV series. Some people remember Frank Sutton, who played Gunnery Sgt. Vince Carter in the TV series *Gomer Pyle USMC*. He began that role in a single episode of *The Andy Griffith Show* in 1964 with a then-virtually unknown singer/actor named Jim Nabors, who starred as Gomer Pyle. The series was a spin-off and was an instant TV favorite for seven seasons, even beating *Star Trek* in the ratings when the latter was moved to Friday nights up against it.

I watched an episode of *Gomer Pyle* on ME TV last night and was blown away by Sutton's acting chops. His role in the series was crucial, and he was a scene-stealer. He was constantly in Gomer's face, yelling, intimidating, insulting, but his roots as a gunnery sergeant

were real. His comedy timing, his movement, his voice, his reactions were all fabulous, and he played that role better than anyone I can think of. But people don't know that "Sgt. Carter," Frank Sutton, was a real Marine. He took part in 14 assault landings on the beaches of the Philippines in World War II. He was honorably discharged following the war, and was somewhat his own "technical advisor" on the series that filmed many scenes at the actual Camp Pendleton in California.

In some scenes the Marines used real ammunition in drills. Yet the show never mentioned the unpopular war in Vietnam that was raging at the time. Sutton was a serious actor who mostly worked in drama. He studied theatre and acting at Columbia University. He appeared in the Academy Award-winning film *Marty* in a supporting role, which led to parts in TV shows like *Naked City, Twilight Zone, The Greatest Show on Earth,* and dozens of others.

Sutton had never performed comedy before, but *Gomer Pyle* was an iconic comedy sitcom for its time. Off screen he was close friends with Nabors, who was gay and closeted because in that era it was a deep secret for any working actor to acknowledge his homosexuality. Married with two children, Sutton was loyal and supportive of his friend, and the two appeared together in Nabors' variety show too, along with fellow *Gomer* actor Ronnie Schell. Nabors remembered Sutton fondly and considered him one of the most compassionate, thoughtful people he had ever worked with. When the series ended Sutton had become somewhat typecast (as had Nabors), and began a tour of musical comedy around 1971.

In 1974, when rehearsing a scene for a musical called *Luv in Shreveport* at a Louisiana dinner theatre, Sutton was stricken with a fatal heart attack on stage. He was just 51 years old.

A Bit More Than a One-Hit Wonder

When I was in college I was a deejay at the University of Miami radio station, WVUM. There was a new record out (you remember records, don't you?) called "Piano Man." I found the singer's voice and style to be a little like Harry Chapin's, though not as interesting an artist.

Since it was Billy Joel's only song on the charts, the crowd that came to hear him on campus one night was small. He performed it early in his set and a lot of people left. I didn't because I couldn't. I had to drive him back to the airport following a radio interview.

He was an interesting guy to talk to and sounded like a lot of New Yorkers I knew as a kid. He was funny and had some great takes on the music business. He was even a rock and roll critic for *Crawdaddy* magazine, long since gone.

When I dropped him off I wished him good luck, thinking, "There's a one-hit wonder if I ever heard one."

Then I listened to the *Piano Man* album. And I realized this guy was special.

First, he had all kinds of styles, including a Copland-esque song called "Billy the Kid," which was an interesting juxtaposition of faux history that he turned into a humorous reference to himself. (Later I discovered that none of the lyrics were historically accurate) Instead of a "six gun in his hand," this Billy the Kid had a "six pack in his hand."

Interesting, I thought. I started following Billy Martin Joel's career closely. Album after album was released: Billy Joel was clearly no one-hit wonder.

Billy Joel is 70 years old now. His is perhaps the most prolific catalogue of American singer-songwriters in history.

Billy told *Rolling Stone* that reaching 70 is amazing enough on its own, but to still perform (he plays monthly at Madison Square Garden) and have people come to hear his hits after almost half a century in the music business still astonishes him.

I don't know how much of a party I deserve just for making it to 70. I mean, it's a work night ... you can't have birthday cake, you can't do any of that stuff.

Still, 70 is a milestone. This is a Peter Pan kinda job. You start out, and you're young, and you're rockin' and rollin', and that's what you do all your life. You become a little myopic about how old you actually are. I see pictures of myself at the Garden recently, and I go, 'That don't look right.' I got old, I lost my hair. I was never a matinee idol to begin with, and there I am on stage still doing the same job I was doing when I was 16.

I've gone on stage and said, 'I don't have anything new for you, so we're just going to play the old shit,' And the audience goes, 'Yeah!' I'll be sitting in the stadium looking out at 30,000, 40,000, 50,000 people, thinking, 'What the hell are they all doing here? Why now?'

I guess, in a way I'm an anachronism. There aren't that many of me left. There's a rarity to it, which gives it value.

Billy Joel has had 33 hit records, mostly Top 10 smashes, and has played most of them thousands of times before audiences ... but never *all* the hits in one show.

Until one night recently.

'Thirty-three hits? That's more songs than we do in a show,' I said. 'Why don't we do a show which is just hits, without album tracks?' And that's what we did the last time, and it's the first time I ever did it.

It was kinda different for us. But I kinda like just going bang, bang, bang, bang, hit, hit, hit, hit. By the end of the show, 'Hey, that was a pretty good set list.'

Pretty good? Well, quite a bit more than pretty good.

I think some of Billy's greatest songs are more than hit records: they've become American treasures. One I've always admired has the feel of an old Drifters tune, from his album of the same name, *An Innocent Man*.

It's a song about the courage it takes and the terror that comes with loving someone. It has meant a lot to me personally.

Some people live far away from the door
if there's a chance of it opening up.
They hear a voice in the hall outside
and hope that it just passes by.
Some people live with the fear of a touch
in the anger of having been a fool,
they will not listen to anyone
so that nobody tells them a lie

I think right there are some terrific lyrics and sentiments.

There are thousands of great lyrics and melodies Billy has created over the years, but to me *An Innocent Man*—far from his biggest hit record—resonates, along with songs like "Vienna," "Summer Highland Falls,""Where's the Orchestra?" and his beautiful "And So It Goes."

I actually think that for his hundreds of millions of record sales and millions of fans, Billy Joel is still somehow underrated as a songwriter and lyricist.

In the print business people make a profession of putting successful artists down. Robert Hilburn, formerly of the *LA Times*, savaged Billy. But nearly 50 years later the songs don't just survive, but live in his fans' hearts and souls.

Billy Joel isn't a very political artist. He rarely takes a political stand on stage because he feels the audience is there to see him perform, not offer his opinions.

But after Charlottesville, when Donald Trump used the phrase, "Some very fine people on both sides" to describe white supremacists, Billy, who is Jewish and whose family barely escaped the Nazis … had enough.

He walked onto the Garden stage wearing a yellow Star of David.

I was pissed off. It's bullshit. There's no fine Nazis. My father's generation fought a war to put an end to Nazism. When they see these guys with the swastika armband, I'm amazed they don't run out on the street and smash them over the head with a base-

ball bat. So this president missed the boat. He had a great chance to say something meaningful and he blew it.

I was never prouder to be a Billy Joel fan.

I always thought Billy would be a very fine novelist, but his literary career began and ended when a publisher wanted him to write his autobiography.

I don't have enough objectivity to do that. There wasn't enough sex, drugs and rock & roll in it for the publisher, so I gave the advance money back. I said, 'Fuck it, that's me.' I don't know if I'm interesting enough to make a movie out of. I lived my life. I don't want to be redundant.

Billy's had bouts with alcoholism and serious drug use. He once admitted he tried heroin, but is clean and sober, in part thanks to Elton John, also a recovering alcoholic.

Before I knew Elton (they've played dual concerts for five years) *I kinda dismissed him as a "Diva Queen." He got me to stop drinking and using drugs, and probably saved my life. I'll always love him and be grateful to him for that.*

Billy Joel has produced and recorded some 15 albums. He's been honored with some of the most important awards any artist can achieve. After almost 50 years in people's consciousness, Billy isn't about to start a farewell tour.

No. I think the way it'll happen is there'll be a night where I feel like I can't do it well anymore ... I can't hit the notes, I don't have the physical stamina, I'm not into it. And that night I'll know it's time to stop. I might even decide right then and there this is my last show. Although my agent will come up to me afterward, 'Oh, no! We can make a lot of money if you do more shows now.'

I hope you had a happy 70th birthday, William Martin Joel. I know you wouldn't remember the kid who drove you to the airport all those years ago. But I'll always have the memory of what you said when I asked you if you wanted to be a star.

"What is a star?" you said. "It's just a ball of gas."

Hardly.

But what a ball ... and a gas we had all these years.

A New Day in Politics

Recently I spent my morning on the phone with one of the most interesting and heroic people I could ever hope to know. Her name is Danica Roem, the nation's first openly transgender state legislator elected recently in Prince William County, Virginia.

For 28 years of her life she said she felt a "hand around her throat"—her own. From the time she was in the 5th grade, Danica told me she knew she wasn't a man. She was a woman in a man's body. For years she said she never fit into any group, didn't feel she belonged to her gender, and wasn't sure if she could even live her life without regret and longing. And yet growing up, Danica had lots of friends, and it's easy to see why.

Danica is a very, very engaging and compelling person to talk to. Not a single friend abandoned her when she transitioned into a woman. She is one run-on sentence after another, witty, smart as a whip, and has so much to say and says what she feels in a thoughtful, uncompromising way. She is a born leader. Some might recoil at her, or dismiss her, or even ridicule her. Danica doesn't much care what anyone thinks of who she is and what she chose to become. But she will fight for the disenfranchised and the marginalized and the people on the edges of society, because she was one of them.

What is interesting is that Roem didn't run with the transgender issue as her key platform. And yet she still had to overcome an opponent who refused to call her by the new gender name that was validated by a judge. She defeated anti-LGBT Republican Bob Marshall, who had held the office for the past 25 years, in one of the nastiest political races Virginia has ever seen. A self-proclaimed "homophobe-in-chief," Marshall was the sponsor of the anti-LGBTQ "bathroom bill." But voters saw through the hate and listened to Danica's ideas and her commitment to serve her constituents. They voted her in.

This metal-loving journalist and stepmom believes she has a passion for leading, but has no deep ambition to run for higher office. She wants to serve her constituents and can speak knowledgeably about toll bridges and taxes, financing public works programs, and policy and infrastructure. She doesn't only want to be known as the first openly transgender legislator in America. Just being Danica is fine with her, and she got immediately to work.

But a look back at her struggles in life shows a deep determination to overcome adversity. Her father committed suicide when she was just three years old and she was raised by her grandfather. When she became a teenager she would pluck out facial hair with a tweezers one at a time. Even though it was painful and inconvenient she felt she needed to be genuine, and was willing to endure anything that came her way to live her life with indisputable authenticity. And so she began enduring painful hormone therapies and processes.

"Gender is how you perceive yourself as your soul; it's only your body and no one else's."

And so on her 30th birthday, just a few years ago, she came "out." She doesn't like to change her voice to seem more feminine to the public, but it's higher now than when she was a man. But Danica pressed on. She juggled three jobs as a journalist while transitioning into a woman.

She has never used drugs. Never smoked a cigarette. And though she once felt she could relate better with an alcohol "buzz," she has also since quit drinking. She traveled to Scotland and Ireland and found friends there who had no issues with her gender identity. They accepted her for who she was. She shared her love of metal music, garish clothes, and great conversation.

Danica Roem had had a busy day. She'd appeared on three MS-NBC shows, the CBS morning show, and was busy answering emails from her constituents. She says she feels exhausted for now but grateful the voters in Virginia gave her an opportunity to make a difference in her district. I asked her what she thought about Trump, and she had a surprising answer in the face of Trump's attempted ban (since blocked) to deny transgenders the opportunity to serve in the military.

She didn't want to talk about that. She wanted to talk about his failure to make good on his promise to spend a trillion dollars in an infrastructure bill. "We need to have improved roads and bridges, and fix the crumbling buildings and schools. We can do better. We have to."

I'm sure there are many who read this who will never accept the person Danica Roem became. But trust me, one conversation with her and you can tell this is a person with passion, conviction, and an undying desire to improve the lives of her constituents and make a positive impact on society. I have several transgender friends in my life and all of them are remarkable people. I have a new friend in Danica Roem, and she told me something that I will take to the grave.

"Never ever let anyone dictate your life. It's yours and only yours. What you do with your life is based on choice and the courage to see your dreams come true."

Danica has done that. The late Nora Ephron once said this: "Above all, be the heroine of your life, not the victim."

Danica Roem wasn't comfortable being a victim. She chose to be true to herself, and for that she is someone I will always deeply admire.

Holy Cow!

Okay, here's another Elvis story, because I just remembered it and it has nothing to do with me.

Harry Caray, the legendary baseball announcer, was broadcasting an NBA exhibition game once in Memphis. (Harry did broadcast basketball for the St. Louis Hawks). Before the game Harry was taking a nap when the phone rang.

"Hello?" said Harry.

"Hello, Harry, this is Elvis Presley, and I'm a big fan of the Hawks and-."

Before he could finish the sentence, Harry hung up. Some idiot is pranking me, he thought. The phone rings again.

"Harry, it's really me ... Elvis Presley."

Harry says, "Listen pal, if you're really Elvis Presley, why not come to the hotel and prove it?"

Elvis told him to watch for a limo out his window in twenty minutes.

Twenty minutes or so go by: a massive white limo pulls up and Harry's eyes pop out of his head.

He races downstairs and runs to the limo. Window rolls down. It's Elvis. He smiles and motions and Harry gets in. Elvis tells him he's been a fan of basketball and a fan of the Cardinals and was also a big Harry fan.

Harry tells Elvis: "Elvis, why not come to the basketball game tonight and sit with me on the broadcast?"

Elvis replies, "Harry, if I go to the game ... there won't be a game."

But then Elvis adds, "But I'll have a limo pick you up ten minutes after and take you to Graceland."

Sure enough, the game ends and it's near midnight, and the car is there. Harry gets in and it drives him to Graceland, where Elvis is waiting with his "Memphis Mafia." Elvis asks if Harry has eaten. Harry says no. Elvis then has his staff order a boatload of fried chicken, BBQ, mashed potatoes, and pies and cakes from the most famous BBQ in Memphis. For the next six hours Harry tells Elvis Stan Musial stories and other sportsl stories... and Elvis loves every minute of it.

A few years go by and Harry is in Las Vegas. Elvis is headlining. Harry gets word to Elvis that he's there, and Elvis sends a note to Harry before the show to come backstage afterward. For the rest of the night—and again until the wee hours—Harry and Elvis hang out together and bond.

Harry Caray and Elvis Presley became instant friends, and remained close until Elvis died. Holy Cow!!!

Here's another Harry story that's amazing in quite a different way. And this one I was there to witness firsthand:

One night many years ago I was in the booth with Harry Caray and former major leaguer Cub announcer Steve Stone. The Cubs were playing the Dodgers and Hideo Nomo was pitching for the Dodgers.

Out of nowhere, Harry, as was his style, wondered out loud if Nomo had an "advantage on his move to first base because he has slanted eyes."

Nomo is clearly Asian.

Steve and I both looked at Harry as if he had a career death wish.

Because even if you believe something so misguided, *you can't say that on radio or TV!*

He repeated it with a small qualifier. "I know some people might be offended by that comment, and I don't mean any harm. I just wonder if there's an advantage."

We tried to get Harry off the subject, but he kept talking about it for the rest of the inning.

Was the damage done?

Well, there was an uproar, but nothing like it would be today.

Harry had to apologize to his listeners and even brought on his friend, the Cubs equipment manager, who was also Asian.

His name was Yosh Kuwano and his brother was Nobe Kuwano, who held the same job for the Dodgers. As kids both brothers had lived in Japanese internment camps.

Yosh was *not* offended. I'm paraphrasing here, but basically what he said was that Harry Caray was no racist, that he was his friend and that that sort of comment, though very awkward and indelicate—and outwardly racist—was just "Harry being Harry."

Things eventually simmered down. But I recalled the incident recently, as the Supreme Court ruled that offensive terms, slurs and slang are protected with trademark as "free speech."

That wouldn't apply here.

I knew Harry well. He was as old-school as it gets but was not a person who wished anyone any harm.

Today he would've been fired within 48 hours. Sponsors certainly would have pulled ads from the broadcast.

Is this a better time?

Yes and no.

We are more aware, more sensitive to ignorance and hate speech, and many jobs have been lost over comments that have been viewed as offensive ... in some cases rightly so.

But to me here's the question that should dictate judgment on unfortunate observations: Is the person uttering the remark *intending* it to be incendiary or hateful? Or as in Harry's case, is the comment ignorant, awkward and insensitive, but *not* intended to be hateful?

Our freedom of speech must be protected. But so too must freedom of thought.

I believe hate speech fuels violence and promotes more hate and should be met with rejection. But ignorance is a gray area for me.

I'm glad Harry kept his job. Cubs fans were too.

Ignorance should be addressed and never promoted. But I don't believe it should cost anyone their job.

Happiness

I believe that happiness is a kind of personal responsibility. When people are happy, everyone around them is sustained and uplifted by that happiness. Conversely, when people exude misery and resentment at every turn, people in their universe are dragged down by them. Money and good fortune never guarantee happiness.

"Pain is inevitable, but suffering is optional."

The person who told me that quote was a man who lived with ALS for decades. He was one of the most positive people I've ever met. His name was Charlie Wedemeyer, a former football player at Michigan State and coach at Los Gatos High School in California. The man couldn't speak. He couldn't breathe on his own. He communicated by blinking his eyes. He lived with ALS and finally died at the age of 64 after 30 of years living with the most confining and paralyzing existence. I believe he lived that long because he felt he had a purpose. He wanted to inspire others, and *he* wanted to show the power of happiness and goodness.

If your life sucks, find something about it that inspires and uplifts you and others. I've met a ton of wealthy and successful people who are miserable. I've met humble and financially challenged people who find joy in their everyday experiences. Love has a lot to do with it. Self love. Love of life.

I travel around the country performing shows about my life in sports and the people I've met. There's one quote that I like to hang my hat on. It's this:

"There's a difference between success and happiness. Success is getting what you want. Happiness is wanting what you have."

I hope you strive for both, but personal satisfaction is more important than affluence and achievement. Happiness and gratitude power the universe. If you don't have either, people won't want to be around you. If you *do* have both qualities, you can light the world.

Tony On the Front Lines

When doing my live show in San Francisco, my favorite city in America, I was walking on Nob Hill and saw a fabulous 8-foot tall statue of Tony Bennett. It had been unveiled just a few years ago for Tony's 90th birthday.

As most everyone knows, Tony is *not* from San Francisco (he's from Queens, New York), but he is an adopted favorite son. It's all because of the song "I Left My Heart in San Francisco." He sings it every single night, with the house lights ... *on!*

It's almost like the Tony Bennett National Anthem. Sometimes audiences actually stand up when he starts.

The song was written in 1961 by George Cory and Doug Cross, and was offered to, of all people, Tennessee Ernie Ford. Can you imagine Ernie Ford associated with that song?

Neither can I.

Ernie turned it down.

Here's a powerful Tony story that might surprise you. Some people knock social activism by celebrities. I don't. Not if it's authentic.

What many folks don't know is that Tony was an early and strong supporter of the civil rights movement—back when it was deeply unpopular for a celebrity to speak out.

He was close friends with Dr. Martin Luther King Jr., having been introduced by his friend Harry Belafonte. A month before King was killed, Tony marched along with him in Selma, Alabama. He had a profound reason for being there that day in 1968.

Three years earlier he'd befriended a woman named Viola Liuzzo, a Unitarian Universalist civil rights activist from Michigan.

In March of 1965, Liuzzo, then a housewife and mother of five with a history of local activism, heeded Dr. King's call. In the wake of the Bloody Sunday attempt to march across the Edmund Pettus Bridge, she decided to leave her home in Detroit and go down to Selma to join the protestors.

She was part of the successful Selma to Montgomery marches and helped with coordination and logistics. Tony was there too, but after a couple of days had to leave for a performance. Liuzzo was the one to drive him to the airport.

On the way back to town Liuzzo was shot dead by members of the Ku Klux Klan. She was 39 years old.

Tony Bennett never got over that tragedy. Civil rights remains one of his guiding principles to this day.

A Girl Named Gloria

Back in the late 60s and early 70s, I used to perform my very limited stand-up comedy act all over Miami Beach, where I grew up. I didn't have much of an act but I could sing and do impressions. I still do it all over the country, but that's another story.

Some down there still remember when I did impressions and sang in school pageants in junior high and high school.

Anyway, when I was about 16 I was hired to MC the talent show portion at a *quinceañera* in South Miami—akin to a Sweet 16 party for Hispanic girls. I think I was paid all of 10 bucks. Again, I wasn't very good, but I had a lot of nerve to get up there and perform. There was one 13-year-old girl on the bill and her name was Gloria Garcia. She had a very solid young person's voice and danced well too. She was a smash that night, and I would later see her occasionally at

clubs, notably when she was about 17 or so at a disco called "Honey for the Bears" in Coconut Grove (a hip neighborhood near downtown Miami).

The years passed and I wondered if that little girl would ever go on to bigger and better things. Then in the 1980s I saw her face on a record album called *Miami Sound Machine*. Under her married name Gloria Garcia would grow to become one of the biggest stars in popular music: Gloria Estefan.

Although she sometimes sings in special shows here and there, Gloria is mainly retired now. Her husband Emilio, also a Cuban American, managed and produced her albums as well as other top artists and recordings, including Jon Seceda, the Latin Grammys and the Spanish version of "We Are The World". Today Gloria and Emilio are worth half a billion dollars, and they even own a piece of the Miami Dolphins.

In the early 1990s I finally caught up with that little girl I had MC'd for all those years ago. She was as kind and humble and generous as she was as a little kid. She and Emilio own a Broadway show that is breaking box office records all over New York and elsewhere. It's called *Get On Your Feet*. And in 2017 she became the first Cuban American to be awarded a Kennedy Center Honor.

I can't wait to see the show, and I have a special place in my heart for that little girl named Gloria Garcia, whom I introduced at that party so long ago.

Ya did good Gloria!

Beatlemania Kills

On Dec. 7, 1980, James Taylor was approached by a man as he left the subway at 72nd street in New York City. The man was sweating profusely and rambling about how he needed to meet John Lennon and wanted to give him something. Taylor quickly dismissed it and got away from the man, figuring he was some kook.

While on the phone the next night, Taylor, who lived next door to the Dakota (the iconic home of many celebrities), heard five shots. That shooter was Mark David Chapman—the same man James had seen outside the subway—and the victim was John Lennon.

It's a chilling and eerie story, but Taylor told the BBC that in some ways, gigantic fame can turn against you professionally and personally.

There's a point of diminishing returns on fame and success. There comes a point where you can't do your job anymore. You are maintaining the form that you have created, that you've been 'cast in.' The odds increase that some crazy person would want a piece of what you represent to them. The greatest artists like John Lennon carry on, or try to, and go far beyond what is expected of them. John tried to keep one step ahead of what the public perceived him to be.

John Lennon had lived quietly for five years raising a son and living a "normal," uneventful, and safe life. Madness mixed with his fame may have cost him his life. Maybe "Beatlemania" was just "mania" in disguise.

Mr. Wonderful

He never attended college, or high school. For that matter, he never attended grade school or kindergarten either.

From the age of three he learned his lessons on the road as a stage performer.

For most of his life he could only write at a second grade level. He ate in segregated restaurants and slept in segregated boarding facilities.

In the army he endured hateful people who urinated in his beer before serving it, where he was called the "N-word" hundreds of times, and was beaten up with regularity.

Like other black performers, on many occasions he still had to perform for white audiences "in blackface."

He once had his car covered in feces. Later, as a public figure, he put up with hate mail and death threats. Even when he became the most versatile performer in American history, he was shunned by the president. He was told that he couldn't date or marry a white woman and still keep his job with a major film studio.

He could sing better than just about anyone.

He could play nine instruments exceptionally well.

He could impersonate dozens of celebrities.

No one could match him as a tap and jazz dancer.

He was expertly skilled at performing tricks with revolvers.

Along with Michael Jackson he was possibly the greatest all around talent in American show biz history. His name was Sammy Davis Jr.

I had the pleasure and honor of previewing a brilliant documentary of the life and times of this American treasure called *I've Gotta Be Me*. It was directed and produced by Sam Pollard, who also gave us the civil rights documentary series, *The Eyes on the Prize*. In the film we learn the Sammy Davis Jr. bore the brunt of a racist America who applauded him, cheered him, toasted him, loved and admired him ... even as he still couldn't even eat or sleep in the same places those people did.

We watch his "Rat Pack" experiences with Sinatra, Martin, Lawford and Bishop, and the fun he had while entertaining in Las Vegas. But still he wasn't even permitted to walk on the Las Vegas Strip.

As I have mentioned many times, Sammy Davis was my childhood performing hero. His celebrity impressions on *The Danny Thomas Show* inspired me to impersonate famous people too.

I loved that we had the same birthday. Every time he came on TV I was glued to the set.

I loved that he could do so many things well and seemed to be having a great time doing them. Yet I never really understood—could never understand—the pain he felt simply living in America.

Sammy Davis Jr. wasn't perhaps just the greatest performer in American history. He was an early civil rights activist who marched on Washington with Dr. Martin Luther King Jr. and walked arm in arm with him in Selma.

He sold out theaters and Broadway appearances throughout his life. And yet so many of his own race called him a "sellout."

I was there the night he hugged Richard Nixon onstage at Miami Marine Stadium. I knew at that moment that he would be heavily criticized, isolated, and ridiculed by his own race. I was sadly correct.

In a way the documentary shows that as beloved as he was, and wealthy as he became (ironically, he died virtually broke), and how admired his legend was ... Sammy Davis never was really accepted by many black Americans. This film does not avoid talking about that.

I've Gotta Be Me is a fascinating but bittersweet film.

I had one of his closest friends, Jerry Lewis, on my show just hours before Sammy died. He told me that Sammy's greatness would never be duplicated, and that the scars Sammy lived with would never be truly healed in America.

Sammy was an American treasure, but he was also an American tragedy.

Only once did I get to meet him, and it was so brief. He was congratulating me for winning some award. I wish I had just thanked him for all he brought to the stage, and the civil rights movement, and for all that he endured while standing tall.

He was Sammy.

Cheered, ridiculed, beloved, ostracized, rewarded, isolated, admired, and despised.

I've Gotta Be Me is the name of the film. The story is an American one filled with shame and glory.

It's Sammy's story, and in many ways it's our story, too.

Bernie and Bernie

Sometime in the 1980s I went to a party at the house of a famous singer-songwriter, and I brought my dad. As I walked around I saw him in rapt conversation with a stranger who was heavily into the Los Angeles Dodgers. My father was a knowledgeable and passionate baseball fan and his name was Bernie. He spotted me and yelled over to me.

"Hey Roy, my new friend's name is Bernie too, and he's really into baseball. He 'claims' to have been a lyricist, but I've never heard of him. What's your last name again, Bernie?"

"Taupin," he said. *It was THE Bernie Taupin... and he'd become fast friends with Bernie Firestone!*

I was reminded of this when I saw Taupin sitting next to Elton John during a Grammy salute on CBS. He's written lyrics to nearly every major Elton John song, and they've been at it for 50 years. What's incredible about their collaboration is that Bernie usually writes his lyrics first and then Elton writes a melody around it. For a long time Elton would bring the lyrics to a recording session, and **on the spot** come up with a melody right then and there—while musicians were on the clock and the meter was running.

In 1972 Elton needed a hair dryer and some sequins sewn into a costume. He knew a woman named Maxine and invited her to become the "seamstress for the band" on tour. Bernie Taupin met her, fell in love with her, and on the spot wrote these lyrics:

"Blue Jean baby, LA lady, seamstress for the band."

You may know the rest of the lyric from "Tiny Dancer."

They married, but it didn't last. But Elton and Bernie have had an artistic relationship and close friendship that has stood the test of time. Yet it started by the most serendipitous of accidents.

In 1967 Elton John was a nobody who could write melodies. He went to a music publisher and said, "I can write songs but I have no clue how to write lyrics."

The publisher replied, "I have hundreds of lyricists who need a melody writer."

He grabbed a box containing the names of those hundreds and pulled the first name, almost literally out of a hat. And that first and only name he pulled ... was Taupin's.

One of the greatest relationships in songwriting history began with "kismet" ... a fortuitous random selection. 800 million dollars and scores of pop hits later *and they're still standing.*

Fourword

Brett Favre and I have always gotten along. I like his "good ol' boy" personality and "aw shucks" demeanor and have been honored to host a few of his Brett Favre Fourward Foundation fundraisers in Mississippi. Brett and I have always shared a fun, candid relationship. His admission that he spent some of his Hall of Fame career in drug rehab did not surprise me. Some years ago he spoke openly about it to me.

"Let me tell you how bad it was with drugs and alcohol," Brett said. "I would drink five or six beers and swallow between 10 and 15 Vicodin every day. One night I threw up and fished the Vike capsules out of my vomit and popped them back in my mouth to make sure I got high again."

Brett would tell me stories of his intoxicated periods, of running stop signs with impunity in Green Bay.

"I felt I was invulnerable and nothing would stop me," he said. "I'm lucky I wasn't killed."

Brett Favre is a good guy who has done some wonderful things (anonymously) for kids and for my charity too. I am a big fan of his and his wife Deanna, and I loved Brett's late dad, Irv, and his mom, Bonita.

But when I think of what *could've* happened to him without drug and alcohol intervention, it gives me a chill. Brett might've been, at one point, the most beloved player in the game. He had some transgressions that today might've cost him his career, but I'm glad he's sober and healthy and enjoying a happy life in retirement with his two daughters and family.

He's earned it.

The Song You Only Think You Knew

To me it's one of the seminal recordings and most recognizable opening in rock history. The song is called "Layla" and it was written by Eric Clapton and Jim Gordon. The first seven bars are among the most important notes in the history of the genre. You know it. We all do.

But here are some interesting things about the song.

First, Eric Clapton *did not* play those seven bars at the start of the record ... Duane Allman did. The legendary guitarist was sitting in with Clapton when he offered that 7-bar riff. It was one of his last guitar licks on record: Allman was killed in a motorcycle accident about six months after "Layla" was released.

Also, many Beatles fans know that the song was, at least in part, dedicated to Clapton's then-girlfriend and eventual wife Patti Boyd. She'd been married to George Harrison, and her affair with Clapton was a part of the "inspiration." But the true inspiration for this iconic song was a 7th-century Arabian lovers tale that later formed the basis of *The Story of Layla and Majnun* by the 12th-century Persian poet Nizami Ganjavi, a copy of which Clapton's friend Ian Dallas had given to him.

Jim Gordon wrote the second half of the song that was something of a piano ballad that Clapton played along with. (Gordon suffered from schizophrenia and was sent to prison after murdering his own mother.)

As far as George Harrison was concerned, not only wasn't he bitter about his best friend having an affair with his wife, he later attended their wedding along with Paul and Ringo.

The song was produced by the legendary Tom Dowd—who also produced hundreds of top records for Ray Charles, Bobby Darin, and dozens of jazz and rock legends.

What's fascinating to me is that Dowd was also one of the physicists who worked on the Manhattan Project helping to develop the atomic bomb.

A classic rock song ... with perhaps a not-so-classic backstory.

Regina

She never graduated college and never had her name in the paper until it came in an obituary. She never wrote the great American novel or achieved any kind of notoriety or fame. And yet she was the greatest woman in my life. The greatest woman in my world.

She led with her heart, always. Kindness came easily to her. Compassion and empathy were second nature.

Sometimes she'd say impulsive things, and some of those may have hurt someone by their bluntness. But she never intentionally harmed another human being in her life, and if she'd known she had she would have been horrified.

The greatest woman in my life hasn't been with us for twenty years, but her greatness was defined by her gigantic heart, her love for humanity, and her intrinsic goodness.

I never knew a more beloved person than my mother.

She was a person who would strike up conversations with perfect strangers ... never self-conscious or cynical was she. In fact I don't think she ever said a derisive thing in her life. She just exuded love to her family and to anyone who knew her.

Once, a long time ago, she offered her home to a stranger she'd met on a plane. That turned out not to be such a good idea. This stranger robbed her of much of her jewelry. When she found out my mom was heartbroken ... not because her valuables had been stolen but because she was dealt a blow in her regard for humanity. My mom trusted people, and though some might have called her naive she was more generous and caring than she was wide-eyed. Her heart grieved briefly, but then she went back to giving.

Anything she had, she offered to the world. Material things, words of comfort and a laugh that was her signature. *What a laugh!* A high-pitched cackle that made everybody laugh along with her. The world was a better place when my mom was here.

I remember she once drove across town to give service station attendants sweaters and hot chocolate on a cold night. She thought they'd need it.

We all needed what she brought us, every day. A cheerfulness, a bright light, a warm heart, and a spirit that I have never seen before or since.

She was never petty or snarky, and never rude. She almost never cursed or offered a dark thought. She was singularly herself, comfortable with who she was, what she had, and what she gave ... to everyone she ever met.

I once wrongly thought she was too "soft" for her own good; I didn't think she was tough enough. Then she got sick with cancer and she showed the world how tough she really was.

She never complained, and actually mocked her disease. She was the last to know she was dying, and it didn't matter because she kept living her life until her dying day with joy, purpose, and that glorious

laugh of hers. Hell, if cancer was a person, she'd have tried to make a friend of it too.

When she died I told her mourners that if you wanted to love my mom you needed to "get in line." The line was long.

No one was ever better at loving and being loved. That was her success. That was her greatness. She wasn't just admired. She was beloved. Anyone who knew her, even on the periphery, could only love her.

Every Mother's Day I remember her. But the truth is, I remember her just about every other day too.

If I have kindness in my heart, and I hope I do, it's come from her. Her sweet gentle soul touched everyone around her.

Recently I watched a show called *Better Things*. There was one scene where the words jumped out at me. It was an adult telling a child about her mother. This is what was said:

Your mother may not be the greatest mother in the world. Sometimes you might laugh at her…even mock her…but she loves you and she would do anything for you. And the most important thing in the world—the most important thing—is that she's there.

You wake up, she's there.

You go to sleep, she's there.

You need her, she's there.

You don't need her, she's there.

Even when she isn't there, she's there.

She will always be there.

And that is all that matters.

That was *my* mom. Always there … until she wasn't anymore. And yet she is indeed "still there" for me and "she will always be there."

Happy Mothers Day to the greatest mother I ever knew.

I only had one mom, and that was more than enough.

Regina.

In Latin it means "Queen" or "Saint".

In any language, she was both.

Yabba-Dabba Don't

Mel Blanc began his career in 1929 performing voices and sounds for early radio. He worked in vaudeville and was also a radio star with Jack Benny. Blanc was the voice of thousands of animated characters and the impetus for me getting into the character voices of celebrities and in movies and TV. He was, among many others, the voice of Barney Rubble.

As a kid I was obsessed with Fred Flintstone. I had scores of pictures, artwork, and other Flintstone mementos in my room.

From the time I was five or six I would often mimic Fred and Barney and other characters and celebrities. My nickname was "Flintstone," and many from my childhood still use it.

When I moved to Los Angeles after being hired by CBS as a sportscaster in 1977, I dreamed of being a voiceover artist for Hanna Barbera, the creators of Fred Flintstone. One day my eventual voice-over agent called me. He had a casting call for a Flintstone project. I was thrilled and terrified at the same time. Here was my dream opportunity: to finally get to lend my voice, even in a small way, to those characters I'd loved as a child. (confession: and still do)

One thing I should tell you. I'm an amateur cartoonist too. I always drew Fred and Barney, and the Jetsons and other Hanna Barbera characters. I still do, and I draw them all well (if I may say so).

I went to the audition and approached the reception desk. Instead of signing my name, I drew Fred. As the casting agent smiled I told her, "If there's any poetic justice in the world, I need to get this job. I'm not doing it for the money, or ego, or anything else. I'm doing this for Fred!"

Over the course of about an hour I hit her with my best stuff.

Finally, with a sweet smile, she told me, "Mr. Firestone, your voices are all wonderful and accurate, but we just don't have a place for them at this time. Thank you, and thanks for the Flintstone cartoon."

I admit I was a little heartbroken. But I was okay with it because at least I had a chance, and failure wasn't the end of the world.

Many years later I got a call. Would I be interested in doing voiceover characters with Mel Blanc (as Bugs Bunny) for a TV show about Bugs and sports? I would be playing Howard Cosell *as a duck!!!*

It would be the very last time Mr. Blanc would perform his iconic voices on network television.

I got to meet and know the sweet genius, Mel Blanc, and still consider this among the greatest honors of my professional career. Mel later invited me to his house on his 80th birthday.

He passed away the next year.

Sometimes life doesn't go the way you want or dream it, but sometimes it works out just fine. It did for me.

"Yabba dabba do!"

The Man With the Golden Pen

Imagine a person so gifted and so talented, and yet equal to that gift and talent possessed of a breathtaking humility, and who practically laughed at all the people who called him the best ever in his field.

I knew that person, and knew him well.

His name was Jim Murray.

He was the finest sports columnist who ever lived, and he was also the funniest and wisest too.

Jim was so self-effacing he once said of his Pulitzer Prize, "Nobody should win a Pulitzer Prize for properly quoting Tommy Lasorda."

But he was wrong. Jim earned it. For parts of six decades, Jim, who wrote for local papers as well as publications like *Sports Illustrated* and *Time magazine*, opined mostly about sports. But people tend to forget he once wrote about crime, politics, and injustice too.

Most of his career he wrote a daily column for the *Los Angeles Times*, and I, along with millions of readers, were treated to his many one liners about sports.

Bons mots like:

I don't know what it is, but I can't look at Hulk Hogan and believe that he's the end result of millions and millions of years of evolution.

The only bad thing about Spokane is that there's nothing to do after 10 ... in the morning.

Willie Mays' glove is where triples go to die.

Golf is the pursuit of the infinite.

Show me a man who is a good loser and I'll show you a man who is playing golf with his boss.

Baseball is a game where a curve is an optical illusion, a screwball can be a pitch or a person, stealing is legal and you can spit anywhere you like except in the umpire's eye or on the ball.

When Mike Tyson gets mad, you don't need a referee, you need a priest.

He was a blend of Oscar Wilde and H.L. Mencken. He was never boastful, never condescended, and could write about anything and anybody, and do it with flair and a signature style. He could break you up with laughter and break your heart with his poignant writing about life.

When he lost sight in one eye he wrote a piece about it, about the "eye" and what his "friend," his eye, was to him.

He referred to his eye as a "he."

Of the eye:

He recorded the happy moments, the miracle of children, the beauty of a Pacific sunset, snowcapped mountains, faces on Christmas morning. He allowed me to hit fly balls to young sons in uniforms two sizes too large, to see a pretty daughter march in halftime parades. He allowed me to see most of the major sports events of our time.

I suppose I should be grateful that he didn't drift away when I was 12 or 15 or 29 but stuck around over 50 years until we had a vault of memories. Still, I'm only human. I'd like to see again, if possible, Rocky Marciano with his nose bleeding, behind on points and the other guy coming.

I guess I would like to see Reggie Jackson with the count 3-and-2 and the series on the line, guessing fastball. I guess I'd like to see Rod Carew with men on first and second and no place to put him, and the pitcher wishing he were standing in the rain someplace, reluctant to let go of the ball.

I'd like to see Stan Musial crouched around a curveball one more time.

I'd like to see Don Drysdale trying to not laugh as a young hitter came up there with both feet in the bucket. I'd like to see Sandy Koufax just once more facing Willie Mays with a no-hitter on the line.

I'd like to see Maury Wills with a big lead against a pitcher with a good move. I'd like to see Roberto Clemente with the ball and a guy trying to go from first to third.

I'd like to see Pete Rose sliding into home headfirst. I'd like once more to see Henry Aaron standing there with that quiet bat, a study in deadliness.

I'd like to see Bob Gibson scowling at a hitter as if he had some nerve just to pick up a bat.

I'd like to see Elroy Hirsch going out for a long one from Bob Waterfield and Johnny Unitas in high-cuts picking apart a zone defense.

I'd like to see Casey Stengel walking to the mound on his gnarled old legs to take a pitcher out, beckoning his gnarled old finger behind his back.

I'd like to see Sugar Ray Robinson or Muhammad Ali giving a recital, a ballet, not a fight.

Also, to be sure, I'd like to see a sky full of stars, moonlight on the water, and yes, the tips of a royal flush peeking out as I fan out a poker hand, and yes, a straight two-foot putt.

Come to think of it, I'm lucky. I saw all of those things. I see them yet.

Jim Murray wrote about triumph in sports, but he also wrote about his personal tragedy.

He lost his beloved wife Gerry, and his son died of a drug overdose. But Jim was a blessed man because following the devastating losses, he met Linda McCoy. She was an angel on earth for Jim, who had lived a solitary and lonely life after those terrible losses. Linda was there to promote him, encourage him, and love him, and she brought his heart back to life.

One night Linda was there when that heart gave out. He died in her arms. They were married only for about three years, but Linda keeps her love, and Jim Murray's love, alive.

Every Monday morning I get an email from Linda Murray. She includes one of Jim's legendary columns and calls it "Mondays with Murray".

Linda too remarried, but for her Jim Murray's legacy is part of her life's calling. She created a scholarship in his name. Currently 31 universities participate annually in a national essay competition in which the winners receive $5,000.

I think about Jim Murray often. I think about his writing, and quips, and insight. And too, I think about the miracle of love between Jim and Linda. I believe she saved Jim's life.

He never lived to see Twitter or Facebook, and likely wouldn't have bothered with them.

But I know this. He was as humble as any man who ever dominated his profession that I have ever known. He once turned down a million dollars to write for a national publication. He didn't think he was worth it. For me he would've been underpaid. Because what Jim Murray represented was more valuable than any amount of money.

He wrote with wit, honor, insight and truth, and about the wonder of life.

How I miss him.

Skipper Chuck

You don't see "kiddie shows" on local TV anymore, and to me that's a sad thing. In their time children's programming and simple fun for little kids on local television was sacrosanct and a priority. Today local news and talkfests swallow up children's access to their own shows on local morning TV.

When I was a little boy in Miami we had a kids' show host named Chuck Zink—known known by virtually every youngster in the county as "Skipper Chuck." I believe Chuck Zink hosted *Popeye's Playhouse* for 30 or more years: never once condescending to children, never once insulting them and their wonder and joy, and never once, even in a private moment, mocking the responsibility adults have, for an hour or so each day, to simply let kids be kids.

Chuck Zink was an immensely talented person. He was an actor, narrator, movie show host, and also hosted the Orange Bowl parade. But his main claim to local fame was as the Skipper.

As was never widely known, Chuck Zink was one of the first Miami broadcast hosts who insisted on integrated audiences. Black, white, and brown-skinned kids were on every show, along with physically-challenged kids. (and don't think he didn't meet resistance in a very racially-segregated city like Miami). Chuck was the local host of the Children's Miracle Network telethon and the Jerry Lewis MD telethon.

One other note:

Chuck was married for about 50 years to Clarice, who had severe emotional problems and several nervous breakdowns. Yet Chuck never abandoned her and never divorced her. He remained steadfast in his loyalty and his love. It was perhaps the most impressive quality of Chuck Zink's life: responsibility and commitment to love.

Once, when I worked at WTVJ in Miami as a young adult, I decided to watch Chuck host the *Playhouse* (which was still taping at five in the afternoon, every afternoon).

After the show was over I introduced myself. I got a bit choked up as I thanked him for his kindness, wisdom, and gentleness to me as a kid who'd had at least three birthday parties on his show.

Without a trace of irony he replied, "It's a pleasure to host shows for kids, and it was a pleasure to host your birthday party. I've hosted hundreds of children's birthday parties for years, and I take the levity and joy very responsibly."

I believe local "kiddie show" hosts like Chuck have great and underrated talents. You're talking to 5-8 year olds and trying to host a broadcast with giveaways, cartoons, and even perform short sketches. To me it's an art form.

Decades passed and Chuck suffered a stroke. The folks at Century Village (a local retirement community) were honoring him and asked me to write and narrate a testimonial. I jumped at the chance.

I thanked him again for his kindness and reminded him of the day I'd praised him (along with so many others of course) for all the good he did for small children as Skipper Chuck.

I got a handwritten letter back, and though the penmanship was a bit shaky, he said he admired me and my work on television. I don't think I've ever got a greater compliment from a total pro, and one of the best broadcasters I've ever known.

Chuck Zink died in 2006, and I still have the letter. What a lot of people don't know is that Chuck was a war hero who earned a Bronze Star in WWII. He was beloved in the Miami community, and to now-grown children there is remembered with warmth and gratitude.

I think it's sad that there are fewer and fewer places for kids to watch a show that teaches character, kindness, and fairness, but that can be goofy too.

Thanks again Chuck for respecting and never patronizing little minds that needed a good and gentle man to "lead the way."

You were one of my broadcast heroes, and I'll never forget you.

Just Say It

A while back I wrote a piece that said in many cases (but not all) gay men are more attractive to women than straight men.

I said gay men appeal to women because, again, (not in every case but often), they love to shop, they tend to be more vulnerable and honest, they love to dress well, they enjoy theatre and sentimental and romantic movies, they laugh easily and live freely, and, (this is important) they are no threat to women sexually.

I realize this sounds like a stereotype, but again, I'm saying that it applies in many, but decidedly not in every case.

Every woman I know has at least one or more gay male friends. There's an ease in many straight woman/gay men relationships that straight guys envy.

You can agree or disagree, but I have another theory that is mostly, but not always, true.

Women are *much* easier with "I love you" than men. That is, they say it to their partners, their girlfriends, their gay male friends, their kids, their parents, and relatives. Guys just can't do it as effortlessly or unconsciously.

"I love you" is almost taboo for men to express, especially in heterosexual relationships.

"I love you" is easier to say for women because I truly believe women love more easily, especially when they trust someone.

Guys are just now getting the "guy hug" down … after all these years. Even the most macho guys can give another guy at least a half-hug now.

We see it more often in sports. The hug is in every greeting among athletes now, though it was almost never so in the 50s and 60s.

But a guy can't easily say "I love you" to another guy. If they say anything at all, it's "love ya man," or some half-baked phrase like that.

There's no authenticity to "Love ya brotha."

Saying "I love you" is terrifying for a guy.

It's vulnerable.

If it's sincere it's almost too intimate.

Bill Walton, who is a dear friend of mine, always tells me he loves me at the end of every conversation. If he stopped saying it, I would think something was wrong. He's never been self-conscious about saying it. I believe he is one of the most content people I've ever met. And "love" does have something to do with it.

My dad once told me he loved me and I almost fell over. He didn't know how to say it to his sons until very late in his life and he figured, "What the hell, it's a good thing to do."

But I always knew what he felt.

My mom said, "I love you," so often it was like her saying hello.

I think that was one of the qualities that really made her great and beloved by others.

I remember the ultimate "man's man," Mickey Mantle, telling me he wished his dad had told him he loved him.

Mickey also regretted not hugging his dad more. When he was a recovering alcoholic Mickey wrote a letter to his long deceased dad, Mutt, telling him he loved him and hoped he loved him back.

That really got me.

Mickey had tears in his eyes when he told me that story.

So did I.

I still get chills remembering that moment.

I heard comedian Mort Sahl once say that the most courageous thing a human being can do in life is to love someone. I think he was on to something. I think this country, this planet, in so many cases is a pretty loveless place. I think we need to say it, feel it, and live it more.

Love, and the expression of it, takes balance, confidence, self-assuredness, and fearlessness.

Guys have a tough time doing it. More and more as I get older, I'm more comfortable telling my friends and family how much I love them. I'm less and less uncomfortable with saying it, and frankly it feels more honest and authentic than one of those stupid phony "white soul" handshakes or high fives.

Love is the ultimate emotion and power in the universe. But for a ton of guys on this planet to say it, show it, express it, is just a scary concept. Next time you're around someone you really do love—a partner, a friend, a parent, and especially your kids—and you know you haven't said it enough, don't say to them, "love ya pal" or "love ya man," tell them in no uncertain terms.

"I love you."

It could feel weird or squishy. It might even be a bit terrifying. But if it's honest, it will feel good.

Because the truth is, I'd rather have gone through my life telling people who matter that I loved them too often than not enough.

I know my mom felt that way. I'm pretty sure my dad would say the same thing if he were around now. Don't postpone joy or love.

And don't be afraid to say it.

Charles the Unpredictable

The biggest, most quotable star in sports broadcasting isn't a play-by-play announcer, or even a studio anchor. He's Charles Barkley, whose unpredictable, outspoken, goofy, and drop-dead quick wit is always entertaining. He earns tens of millions of dollars for his TV analysis and commercials. He's even hosted *Saturday Night Live*.

He is beloved, and sometimes vilified, but usually not for long. Even when he gets into trouble for something he says or does, most people will just smile and shake their head and say, "That's Charles."

I've probably interviewed Charles more than anyone in the business (at last count it was about 25 times). I interviewed him as a player coming out of Auburn, then in the Olympic trials, and then later of course as a player for Philadelphia, Phoenix, and Houston.

Charles Barkley is super witty, but he's sometimes thought of only as controversial and not as an intellect. He may not be well read, but Charles is pretty smart and rational. Of course he has an appetite for saying what he feels and he doesn't hold back on any subject.

Once I asked him if he thought he was going to heaven.

Without missing a beat he replied, "I don't know, but I can tell you it's going to be a close vote."

There aren't many originals in sports anymore. Not in real life either. But Charles is the one and only.

One of my all-time favorite people.

The Price of Fame

Michael Jackson would be more than 60 years old now. It's hard to believe that it's been a decade since he died of an overdose of self-prescribed drugs. I think about who and what he was, what impact he made in the recording and performing arts, and I think about the awe and affection he had inspired around the world. But what if he had just been another kid growing up—one of eight to the Jackson family—and lived his life in his hometown of Gary, Indiana?

Yes, you might say, but the world would've been denied perhaps the greatest entertainer in America's history. His family would've been denied unimaginable wealth and notoriety. But it's likely that were he not famous, with all the inherent pressures and expectations, he would still be alive. And wouldn't have undergone a dozen plastic surgeries, worn disguises in public, and likely would never have needed drugs to dull the fear, anxiety, and pain that went with fame and adulation.

I remember George Harrison once said that being a Beatle "cost him his central nervous system." Michael Jackson, like any global star, had plenty of "yes" men and women, but not enough "no's" in his life.

No, Michael, you *can't* have children in the bed with you. You can't keep doing this to your face. You can't keep buying llamas and giraffes and chimpanzees to keep you company because you want to live your adult life in a childhood you were never really allowed. I believe show business is a wonderful thing to experience, but the crushing burdens, especially to those who have to deliver bigger, better, and more beautiful, are deeply destructive to anyone.

Michael Jackson didn't make it to 60. He didn't make it to 51, for that matter.

Had he not been famous and celebrated, John Lennon wouldn't have been murdered.

Being a celebrity is not such a wonderful life. *You* get to go home after a concert or go on with your life after you hear a song. People like Michael Jackson and others in that stratosphere live with torment, anguish, and emptiness. Fame and expectation is an unquenchable beast that must always be fed. You are exceedingly well paid, and loved and admired all over the world. But to me, it's no life at all.

Women We Love

Esquire magazine used to have a feature dedicated to the "Women We Love."

I don't think it was mean-spirited sexism, but it did reduce women merely to their attractiveness for a mostly male audience. Still, for the sake of discussion, those issues came to mind when I thought of Julia-Louis Dreyfus today. She is absolutely a woman I love. I admire her spunk and snark and playfulness. She's also very beautiful.

I'm sure I'm getting into dangerous territory here, but I'm willing to take a shot at a list of women I've always loved, and though many of these women are physically attractive (and not all in obvious ways), they also all exude something that makes me love and appreciate them.

First, I always have loved women in my life, though I've always been very shy and intimidated by all kinds. I was often overmatched by women with their grace, style, manner, and elegance, because I have none of those qualities.

I love smart, witty, thoughtful, and kind women.

I always thought Elayne Boosler was that kind of person.

Taylor Swift is an extremely talented songwriter who uses her fame and affluence to support many causes. I know personally because Dick Vitale told me she once cut two personal checks on the spot for the Jimmy V Foundation totaling $300,000.

I love Eva Longoria's intelligence and activism.

Alyssa Milano raised $50,000 for South African women and children with AIDS by selling photo work.

Jennifer Garner too. I imagine the every-day tabloid attacks on her are withering, but she somehow keeps moving forward for her dignity and her family's.

I appreciate women who are strong and energetic, and by their sheer determination never manipulated. The women who are always one step ahead of a man in temperament and wisdom.

And women who are wise are usually the greatest women of all … for me.

Anyway, here's a partial list of women I love, most of whom are notables, but not all.

Besides Julia Dreyfus, I love Tina Fey, Sam Bee, and Mary Tyler Moore, Diane Keaton, Sarah Silverman, Amy Sedaris and Teri Garr. In addition to enormous talent they have shown independence, fearlessness, and artistic integrity.

Elizabeth Banks, Sandra Bullock, Melissa McCarthy and Jennifer Lawrence. Funny, smart, and talented, but always leading with their heart.

Carrie Fisher was one of my all time favorite women of notoriety. She was filled with sass and honesty, and she was wickedly funny and sharp-tongued.

I loved Pearl Bailey and Carol Channing too. Bright, dangerously funny, snarky when necessary, but at their core they were kindhearted and humane.

Martina Navratilova and Billie Jean King never disappointed me with their intelligence, wit, and social awareness.

When I interviewed Danica Roem after her victory in the Virginia House of Delegates, winning the Democratic Primary in the 13th District, I became fascinated by her courage and desire to serve. She overcame the stigma and hate toward transgender people, yet she practically never brought up being a transgender American. She wasn't interested in being a symbol. She only wanted to be an effective legislator. She's definitely an unforgettable person, and someone I deeply admire.

I always have deep affection for Bo Derek, but not for the obvious "guy" reasons. She's a lover of horses and rescues animals and has a foundation for both. She's also a lovely person and very unassuming.

Reba McEntire has always struck me as a very good human being with tons of warmth and perspective … Love her.

The two morning show anchors at Fox KTTV in LA where I

contributed for years are terrific women I love … Maria Quiban and Araksya Karapetyan … funny, warm and so kindhearted as well as beautiful.

Lily Tomlin, Meryl Streep, Eleanor Roosevelt, Rosa Parks, Amelia Earhart … some living, some gone … all fascinating and daring and strong.

I loved Chrissy Hynde of the Pretenders, Joni Mitchell, Judy Collins, Susanna Hoff of the Bangles. Linda McCartney was a great human being whom everyone loved, even more than Paul.

I have eternal unrequited love for Linda Ronstadt. Everything about her speaks to valor and intelligence and grace and risk-taking to go with her immense talent, and she never ever complains. These are all musicians as brave, outspoken and daring as they are talented.

I love women like J.K. Rowling, the author of the *Harry Potter* books. She is an extremely humanistic and humane person. I love what she stands for. I love what she writes about. I love the writer Anna Quindlen, who always writes about love and empathy, soul and goodness, and touches my heart with every line. Same with Doris Kearns Goodwin, who just exudes humanity and warmth.

I will always have a special place in my heart for my old friend Connie Chung. We shared much laughter and so much fun. The same goes for another old friend, Ann Curry, who always made me laugh.

I love women in power who have compassion and depth—people like Elizabeth Warren and Barbara Boxer—and now I love Kamala Harris. All of these women have qualities of courage and fearlessness.

A couple of Republican women I loved and love are the late Barbara Bush and Laura Bush, who seem like good-natured and wise human beings.

Of course Michelle Obama is a woman I would love even though I also love and admire her partner, because Michelle seems like a thoughtful, considerate, and bright human being.

I'd vote for her if she ever ran for office … but she's too smart for that.

I loved Phyllis Diller. I interviewed her a few times. She was super-intelligent and well read and was a great person who dreamed big and succeeded in a man's world.

My friend Melissa Manchester knows I will always love her and have for 45 years because of her eye and ear and heart. She's always a great conversationalist and I've had many amazing talks with her.

Women who impressed me included the late Sally Ride, Malala Yousafzai, and Senator Mazie Hirono of Hawaii.

Ella Fitzgerald and Joan Baez are talent and courage and wisdom all rolled into one.

I loved Katerina Witt and Jackie Joyner-Kersey because they were the best at what they did and yet were open and accessible to talk to.

I admire Hillary Clinton and think she's been the most unfairly maligned political figure in my lifetime, but I don't know that I "love" her. She doesn't get into my heart like many other women. She seems very wonky and professorial to me, but I still hold her in high regard.

I love Rachel Maddow. I think she's brilliant and compassionate. She seems to be a wacky person too who doesn't take herself too seriously, but she takes her work extremely seriously. She's the best at what she does in broadcast history.

I have a new love in Nicolle Wallace of MSNBC because she isn't just a solid interviewer and reporter, she can laugh at herself and her world and makes everyone around her at ease.

I love people like Fran Lebowitz and Merrill Markoe and Emma Thompson, and Vanessa Bayer and Cecily Strong and, of course, Kate McKinnon of SNL. Whimsical and droll women, each and every one.

And who didn't love Gilda Radner?

I love Carole King and what her songs say.

Aretha seemed like a formidable and no-nonsense woman. I would like to have known her, but she probably would've been hard to get too close to.

Christie Brinkley looks like a great woman who isn't just beautiful but loves animals and causes; and Beth Stern (who happens to be Howard's wife) because of her generosity to abandoned animals.

The interesting thing about this list is that I don't know and have never met almost all the women. But I have admired all these women.

This list is deeply incomplete, but I would be remiss if I didn't acknowledge my all-time favorite woman ... my mom. She's long gone now, but I loved her grace, and laugh, and easy going manner, and she really, really showed me what love is, and how to live a life with vivacity and joy. And when she was faced with life's greatest challenge, she stared death down with humor and bravery.

Anyway I've gone on too long. I just want people to know, as I've always said, that for me, most women are better than most men I know. Oscar Wilde once said, "Women are to be adored…not understood." I don't pretend to understand all women, but in my life I've adored so many. I love women who make it easy to love them, and so many have … though I always felt in awe of many.

I look forward to all the wonderful women I have yet to meet.

Who are women you admire?

Miles Ahead

People ask me all the time what or who was my most memorable interview. There were so many it's hard to nail down one or two. I can tell you about Miles Davis, the most controversial and elusive interview in jazz circles ever. He famously didn't give many, but he wanted me to interview him. Because he was a massive boxing fan I think he wanted to talk sports. But I had no intention of wasting this golden opportunity: I wanted to talk music.

I spent the day with him and he told me a story that says a great deal about his reluctance to be accepted by mainstream audiences. After a gig one night the actor Peter Graves came into his dressing room. With a puzzled look on his face Graves told him, "Miles, I don't get your music."

To which Miles replied:

"That's good!"

Pure Miles.

Though I didn't know him well, we got along famously that day. And yes, I miss him a lot too.

Just For Laughs

Even though I'm known to many as the "guy who made them cry in an interview," I bet we had more laughs on our show by maybe, oh ... 1,000 to 1, easy.

I believe you should be around people who are easy with a laugh. I never want to work that hard for a laugh, but I also love great and easy audiences. I *love* to hear laughs. Love it.

Some laughs are unforgettable.

My mom's was this staccato, high-pitched, really loud laugh you could hear from a mile away. But it was never obnoxious. My dad's laugh had to be earned, but I had the key to his laugh lock box.

People I love all have great laughs. People I remember with great laughs.

Johnny Carson.

Phyllis Diller (Yes, she really did sound that way off stage when she laughed, and she laughed a lot.)

Tony Gwynn was easy with a laugh. Sometimes it was a cover to mask his anxiety in an interview, but when he laughed it was uncontrollable ... a fit!

I freaking loved Magic Johnson's laugh maybe the most of all.

Believe it or not, Kareem Abdul-Jabbar has a booming, hysterical, unforgettable laugh. I heard it around the Laker locker room when he was in a good mood, which was most of the time.

I loved Dave Letterman's laugh ... even when one of his bits was dying.

Sammy Davis Jr. was a "too-easy" laugher. He felt the need to bring attention to himself even in his laugh. He had to walk away and tap his feet and do convulsions. A definite over-the-top laugher. But

I still love Sammy. He's my hero.

I believe that if your laugh to tears ratio isn't close to 100 to 1 or higher, you're not living the kind of life I'd want. Even though tears are good, I think laughs are better.

Hey, how about laughing so hard you cry?

I've done that, too. Don Rickles on my show was so funny tears were dripping down my face!

Anyway, those are some thoughts on perhaps one of the most important human reactions of all.

Laughter.

Robert Rules

I think the finest and most diverse talent in broadcasting in my generation is Bob Costas.

He's won so many Emmys and Sportscaster of the Year awards, at this point they should just engrave his face on the trophies. Twenty-eight Emmys at last count.

I've known Bob for nearly 40 years. He's a friend who has been supportive and helpful in my career. That's why I made it my business in July of 2018 to fly to Cooperstown, NY, the home of the baseball Hall of Fame, to show my support and admiration for Bob's induction into the broadcast wing with the Ford C. Frick Award.

I joined thousands in the audience—along with his wife Jill and two grown children Taylor and Keith. And even his former wife Randy .

Many of Bob's friends were in attendance. Some came from NBC, some from the MLB Network, some from HBO.

But knowing Bob all these years I thought about one person who wasn't there: the guy who'd introduced Bob to the game, his father John. Their love for baseball was mutual and abiding, but it carried some sadness too. Over the years Bob and I have talked about his father and the thoughts were always bittersweet ... both joyful and sad.

When he stepped to the microphone he briefly alluded to his dad, and how tracking John Costas' baseball bets introduced young Bob to many of the broadcasters he would later join in the profession.

"My first 'reporting' job was to relay the scores to my father and tell him how his bets were going."

As Bob said on that stage at Cooperstown, their father-son relationship was more Daymon Runyon than Norman Rockwell.

My relationship with my father was exhilarating and funny, but also sometimes difficult, and ultimately, unresolved.

I was only 18 and he was 42 when he died of a heart attack in 1970. He never saw anything that I did professionally, so I can only imagine what he would have felt with me up at the podium in Cooperstown. I'd like to think it would be pride and appreciation and enjoyment, but I'm not 100% sure. Even though it was never my objective, being as lucky as I was in broadcasting led to financial security, and maybe that might've taken some of his urge to gamble away. But even then I'm not sure that's even true.

It wasn't as much about the money as it was the exhilaration of winning a bet, or even if he lost ... the exhilaration of the action. I'm left to wonder whether he could even have stopped himself from betting on games that I broadcast! I remember his angry yelling at the TV if the game was going the wrong way. Sometimes he didn't like the tone of the announcers—Chris Schenkel, Lindsay Nelson, Marty Glickman, whoever. If their voices brought him bad news, then he cursed them too. Would he feel that way about his own son? I'll never have the answer to that question."

Bob continued.

You know, I could've turned away from sports. My mother and sister had no use for sports because they associated it with the heartache … and the trauma that was involved with it … the chaos. I connected with sports because I liked it, but also because it was a way to connect with my father, who in his best moments was entertaining and charming, a funny, intelligent, and charismatic guy. I could forgive almost anything when those moments came along, and there were lots of them. At his best he was much more interesting and colorful than the guy next door who mowed his lawn every Saturday.

When I'd go out to the driveway at night and listen for out of town scores on the car radio, I calibrated the dial like a safecracker searching for far off stations and the voices of baseball. If things broke right I could be the bearer of good news. On the other hand, it was particularly difficult when he would bet against the Yankees. As a New York kid, I loved the Yankees. I hung on every Mantle at bat, even in his fading years. I remember Mantle hitting a home run in the bottom of the ninth to win a game when my dad had bet against them. He took his anger out on me because he suspected I was silently more happy that Mantle had homered than I was concerned about the $500 bucks he lost.

He was like a lot of men in his generation who grew up in the Depression and served in the military. Today we tell our kids how much we love them. He'd give me an occasional pat on the head, or "nice job," or "that was good," or maybe a shared laugh. That was his way. He was not a sentimental man.

And yet he was the kind of guy who literally on a July night at midnight would wake me up, shake me out of the bed, and say, "Robert, let's go to Coney Island and get a hot dog at Nathan's. And so we'd drive for an hour to Brooklyn, we'd eat a couple of dogs, and we'd ride the cyclone. The other dads down the street didn't do that.

Speaking of Brooklyn, I was with him once when he collected $14,000 from a bookie in a doughnut shop. I'm on a stool at the counter, with my dad and this guy who looks like he's been sent in from Central Casting: snap brim hat, pinky ring, a gruff exterior.

In his deep Brooklyn accent the guy says: "Is dat your boy? Nice boy" This was followed with: "Give da kid a doughnut and a glass of milk." And then this bookie slid a bag across the counter, matter of factly ... because it was just business to him.

Five minutes later my dad and I are sitting in the car under a street light and he's counting out fourteen grand in $100 dollar bills. In 1966. That was close to how much we paid for our house.

We were essentially "on the lam" when we moved for two years to Redondo Beach, California in 1960. It was an abrupt move. He owed some less-than-forgiving people more dough that he could scrape together. I understand him better now, for better and for worse.

I found Bob's comments about his dad both loving and wistful ... appreciative and yet longing.

But when I asked Bob about his Cooperstown speech, there were no mixed feelings. His love for the game and the profession was never in doubt.

It was an appreciation of the craft and of the people who inspired me, many of whom became friends, and reached out to me and were so gracious ... like Dick Enberg and Vin Scully.

I spoke about the Kirk Gibson home run in the 1988 Series because it illustrated something important about the craft, because even Kirk Gibson remembers that moment through the prism of how it was covered.

As I said, we think of the announcers first and foremost, but if Harry Coyle doesn't direct that moment as perfectly as he did ... and if Mike Weissman and John Fillipelli don't choose the replays as perfectly as they did ... if they don't get Dennis Eckersley craning his neck looking over his left shoulder to follow the ball's flight...Tony LaRussa stalking from the dugout and down the tunnel ... if they don't get Tommy Lasorda jumping in exaltation ... if they don't get Gibson pumping his fist between first and second ... if they don't get him slapping hands with third base coach Joey Amalfitano ... if they don't get Gibson approaching the plate from two angles, behind him and in front of him. The way it all came together, along with Vin Scully's great call, it would NOT be remembered quite the way it is.

In many cases, the way we remember the most resonant moments in sports is shaped by the way those moments were described and covered.

Bobby Thomson's homer is a big deal, but without Russ Hodges' call it doesn't echo down the corridors of time the way it does. Sandy Koufax is Sandy Koufax, but Randy Johnson threw a perfect game.

Don Larsen threw a perfect game in the World Series. What elevates the Koufax perfect game even beyond the perfection on the mound is the perfection of the call in the booth by Vin Scully.

Would they even call it "The Miracle on Ice" if Al Michaels didn't say 'Do you believe in miracles?'

I believe the very best announcers, in their best moments, don't just reflect the excitement but actually shape how we experience…and then remember those moments.

Bob Costas has had not just an immensely storied and decorated career but one of the most diverse ones too. He's been a play-by-play announcer, but he's also an award-winning interviewer on shows like NBC's *Later with Bob Costas*, HBO's *Costas Now* and *Costas on the Record*.

He's also conducted memorable radio interviews on *Costas Coast to Coast*.

I asked if his broadcasting career accurately reflected something that was true of him personally.

Well, I could interview Elie Weisel on the Holocaust one night and take a pie in the face from Soupy Sales the next. I could be on Letterman doing elevator races and then on Meet the Press or Nightline talking about some sports issue that transcended into news.

After 40 years Bob has stepped away from NBC, but he's not retiring.

I asked him about the difference between celebrity and accomplishment, and if he could, would he prefer to work his career in a vacuum without celebrity and its false promises and rewards.

I never lived as a celebrity. I never conducted myself that way. But if I had broadcast in a hypothetical vacuum it would've robbed me of a great blessing, which is appreciation.

I would rather receive appreciation than adulation. So, when someone says, 'Hey, I know you,' or 'Hey, its Bob Costas,' I'm polite to them, but that doesn't mean all that much to me. But if someone actually expresses some understanding, like 'I remember your interview with Robert Duvall on Later' ... I mean, that's more than 25 years ago. Then what you're receiving is genuine appreciation. That matters to me.

Bob has been called a broadcaster who can be reverent and irreverent almost at the same time.He is funny and often biting both in private conversations and on the air. He takes what he does seriously but never confuses seriousness with solemnity.

Many years ago, I asked Baseball Hall of Fame announcer Jack Brickhouse, whose eyesight was failing him, to take a few moments and reflect what his eyes had seen in his career.

I decided to ask Bob the very same question and he grew reflective and specific.

The Ramblas in Barcelona ... walking toward the edge of the Mediterranean at midnight during the 1992 Olympics.

I saw Muhammad Ali lighting the torch in Atlanta in 1996. I saw Michael Jordan's final championship winning shot against Utah in 1998. I saw the anticipation turn to anguish in the blink of an eye in the 6th game of the World Series in 1986.

I was in the Red Sox clubhouse waiting to conduct what appeared to be the first ever World Series post game interview of a Red Sox championship, because even radio barely existed in 1918, the last time they had won. The ball going through Bill Buckner's legs changed it in an instant.

And then two years later, I'm in the corner of the Dodger dugout late in Game One of the World Series and I see Kirk Gibson limp out of the tunnel, and as he eventually heads to the plate. I'm thinking, 'This is something out of a B-movie script. They never would have bought it on paper.' But it came true in reality.

And then being asked to eulogize Mickey Mantle and Stan Musial. What are the odds of this?

It's been an amazing ride for Bob Costas. The "odds" are that John Costas would've been very proud.

Country Puncher

I've had a lot of colorful and quotable people on my show over the years.

Charles Barkley was one. Sir Charles was funny and quick-witted.

Jim Valvano was another. A great storyteller and a human quote machine.

But nobody cracked me up more often and with more original one liners than Randall "Tex" Cobb.

If you followed boxing in the 80s and 90s you might remember Tex. He was a human punching bag. A brawler, and mostly a bleeder. What he lacked in pugilistic skills, Tex made up for in wit.

He was less a fighter like Oscar De La Hoya than a wit like Oscar Wilde. Here are a few of his memorable bons mots:

"If you screw things up in tennis, it's 15-Love. If you screw up in boxing, it's your ass."

Or his assessment of the punching power of Earnie Shavers:

"Earnie Shavers could punch you in the neck and break your ankle."

"Larry Holmes doesn't hit as hard as Earnie Shavers. Nobody hits like Shavers. If anybody hit harder than Shavers, I'd shoot him."

It was the Larry Holmes fight that made Tex famous. He was on the receiving end of a battering at the hands of the champ. It was such a mismatch that Howard Cosell, who was calling the fight, quit on the spot in disgust.

When told that Cosell quit the sport after that Cobb called it "My gift to boxing."

Asked about a possible rematch against Holmes, Tex said:

"I don't think his hands can take the abuse."

Or another time::

"Only if it's held in a phone booth."

Tex had a booming laugh to go with his lightning fast one-liners. His quips became so popular that he was cast in many films and TV shows. And though the medium brought him some success he made his living mainly as a boxer ... though he never put his ego into it.

Here's Tex on Tex:

I've always believed the greatest crime a man can do is to take himself too seriously. Something like fighting is pretty ridiculous to take seriously. What I do is hit people. I'm not promoting anything that is real or valuable. All I want to do is hit somebody in the mouth. It's a whole lot easier than working for a living. Don't make anything noble out of what I do.

Then Tex talked about the democracy of beating people up.

"I'll fight any white man, black man, brown man or man of any other color. I especially like it when they're yellow and having physical or mental breakdowns when they step in the ring."

On being floored for the first time in his life:

"Nah, it didn't affect me. I just got up and carried on with my game plan; stumbling forward, getting hit in the face."

But Cobb was at his wittiest when the subject was Don King:

Don King is one of the great humanitarians of our time. He has risen above that great term "prejudice. He has screwed everybody he has ever been around. Hog, dog or frog, it don't matter to Don. If you got a quarter, he wants the first twenty-six cents.

Tex Cobb had his battles with substance abuse, and in 1999 lost his eldest son Bo in a tragic accident. But Tex, who now lives in Philadelphia, has found a pathway to success outside of the world of boxing.

In January 2008, at age 57, Cobb graduated *magna cum laude* from Temple University with a bachelor's degree in sport and recreation management. He remarked that it was odd to hear the cheers of a packed arena without being in a boxing ring.

"It was nice to have that opportunity to wear a robe, to step up there and not have to worry about bleeding."

The Star

Over the years I had many Hollywood stars on my show *Up Close*, and there were some very big ones. One day a gigantic star even then came on and we were all excited. This star didn't request a limo, because the star didn't like them. Limo drivers were starting to record celebrity chitchat, and besides, this star had a perfectly good exotic car and would do the driving. The car was a Honda Accord that the star had owned for years. This star walked onto our set asking if anyone had change for a parking meter. That's right, this star hadn't even thought to pull into our lot. We laughed and told the star we could park it, but the star didn't care. I fished out a couple of quarters.

This star came back from feeding the meter and did a fantastic interview. This giant star was hysterical, a great storyteller, and warm and friendly to our entire crew. Leaving the studio the star had remembered every camera and lighting person's name, and thanked them for their time. We gave this star a coupon for some custom shirts for appearing on the show.

The star was ... Tom Hanks.

He was promoting *A League of Their Own* directed by the late Penny Marshall, who died in 2018 at 75. He had already starred in numerous hit movies like *Big*, which generated some $100 million, a first for a female director. This would open the door for numerous talented female film directors.

I would see Tom at other functions and we always had funny and random conversations about numerous things, including at a red carpet event I hosted for Muhammad Ali in Phoenix. We kibbitzed for 30 minutes about one of our mutual interests, the Dave Clark 5.

Even after *Philadelphia, Private Ryan, Forrest Gump, Toy Story, Sully,* and a couple of other dozen major films, Tom was still un-affected by fame. Flash to 20 years later. At a red carpet event he walked up to me, and without pretension or prompting thanked me for the two custom shirts. *He still had them in his closet.* He then handed over the two quarters he'd borrowed for the meter.

Tom Hanks: One of the greatest and most decent people I've ever met in show business. And he still doesn't use limos.

The Other Bernie

The two most important men in my life were named Bernie.

My dad was Bernard Firestone, and his influence and love for me were incalculable. The other Bernie is Bernie Rosen, the first sports director on my very first local job in Miami at TV station WTVJ, the CBS affiliate.

My dad's impact on me is represented throughout my life and in this book. So I'd like to devote the next few pages to the remarkable "other" Bernie. Interestingly, the two Bernies never crossed paths and never really knew each other. But because my dad took a massage at the same spa as Bernie Rosen and my dad knew that, he asked his massage therapist to ask Mr. Rosen if he would offer his son Roy an internship at the station.

Bernie Rosen said yes, and that's how my career began.

But let's start with Bernie Rosen's backstory.

In 1949 as a 19 year-old student at the University of Miami, Rosen joined friends Ralph Renick and Bob Weaver as interns at WTVJ, one of the first local TV stations to broadcast in the South. If you grew up in Miami you knew Ralph Renick, a towering figure in the local TV news scene for 35 years—in effect the Walter Cronkite of South Florida. Weaver would also become legendary as "Weaver the Weatherman," a beloved and honored personality for decades.

But Bernie Rosen never wanted to be a broadcaster, and though surely a force in the local scene, he was hardly a household name like Renick or Weaver.

"When I was hired full-time in 1950," said Rosen, "I ran camera. I directed the news. We had a 15-minute broadcast. The station was only on the air for about 6 or 7 hours a day. We had no budget. I remember we would cut pictures out of newspapers or magazines to help visually broadcast the news. I was 18 years old and I was making $50 a month!"

Rosen loved sports and the station knew it, so they gave him the title of "Sports Director," which in the 50's in Miami was like being named "head light bulb changer."

Miami was a vacation capital during the winter. It had no pro sports at all. No Miami Dolphins. No Miami Heat. No major league professional sports like the Marlins or Florida Panthers. So Rosen decided to make local sports coverage a "thing."

"I was just a little kid from the Bronx. I was lucky to afford a sandwich. I went to DeWitt Clinton High School. I didn't know anything back then, but I liked to hustle, and so when I moved down there and went to the University I got a chance to intern, and I just took it upon myself to make this thing go."

There was no money to broadcast sports, so Rosen, who was now up to making $150 a month—most of it going to pay his rent—rode public buses to get to locations to shoot stories.

"We had wind up Bell and Howell cameras, and I would ride busses all over town and shoot track meets, swimming competitions, dog races, hell, even marble tournaments. And God, we shot high school football. A ton of high school football."

Then Bernie found out something he hadn't figured on. Parents and friends of those athletes wanted to see their friends and family on local TV. "They became our viewers," Rosen said. "And they never left us."

For the next six decades ... that's *six* decades ... Bernie Rosen became to Miami TV sports broadcasting what Vince Lombardi was to pro football. Rosen ran the largest local TV sports department in America, and he built championship careers. He helped make national careers of broadcasters, executives, cameramen and producers. Maybe 100 men and women owe their careers to Bernie Rosen and WTVJ. I know because I'm one of them.

The year was 1972. You were a little bit of a scatterbrain. We knew it then Roy, but one of the things I prided myself on was being able to spot people with talent and ability. You were filled with talent but certain things eluded you...like organization. I remember you were so scatterbrained that when you finished covering the Dolphins, you got in the car and drove back to the station. Little did you realize that you left the camera on the hood of the car. They found it on the Julia Tuttle causeway. I could've killed you. And you did the same thing twice!!

Okay, I'll admit I wasn't the most coordinated and methodical cameraman and editor in the history of broadcasting. One time I edited a film clip backwards, so that the anchor was reading a voiceover while a pole vaulter leapt up from the sand pit, flew over the bar and ran backwards to the front of the line in slow motion. I can still see the anchor's face now as I write this. He looked like he'd just seen a ghost!

Bernie Rosen was patient with this 17-year-old kid named Firestone. He slowly showed confidence in me, and later asked me to interview Dolphin Coach Don Shula's 3 a.m. airport arrivial. Waiting for that plane I must have practiced starting the camera and running in front of it to grab the interview 20 times.

Little did I know that this was the playoff game where the Dolphins lost to the Raiders on the last play, so when Shula got off the plane the last thing he wanted to see was some kid with a microphone. It went something like this:

Shula: "What the hell do *you* want?"

Me (terrified): "Oh ... nothing ..."

Shula gave me his famous stone face and I had to tell Bernie Rosen I didn't get the interview. (P.S.: Coach Shula and I later became good friends)

To say Bernie was furious was putting it lightly. Then after he gave me a tongue-lashing he said something I would never forget. "Get the Goddamned interview. Get the story. Don't let anyone tell you no. Insist. Don't ever take the easy way out."

And then he said something else that I still hear in my heart even today.

"If you have ability, no one can take it away from you. But if you don't use your ability, you take it away from yourself."

In my short time at WTVJ I was at the receiving end of a great many of Bernie's lecture. Yet I never forgot his ethic, his demand for doing a job thoroughly and with integrity. I asked Bernie what he was proudest of in his years at the station.

There were many people who meant a lot to me. Some went on to bigger and better things. What made me proud were the thank yous I received, but there were two people who stand out.

Muhammad Ali was a kid who came to Miami in 1960 after winning the Gold medal in the Olympics. We helped him become the personality he would become. He did maybe fifty interviews with us, and he always remembered WTVJ. It was a rough time in Miami back then. Black people were on a curfew. They weren't even permitted to be on Miami Beach after 6pm, if you can believe it. One time Angelo Dundee (Ali's trainer) had to call the police department and tell them that a black kid would be running (doing his road work) on MacArthur Causeway so that they wouldn't arrest him. I remember black people couldn't sit in the stands at the Orange Bowl. They were only allowed in the

216

end zone. We covered Clay before he became Ali, and he always remembered us because we always treated him with respect and affection.

The other area of pride for Rosen was the hiring of the first woman local broadcaster in history, Jane Chastain.

She was a lady. And what Jane went through was horrible. Dolphin Coach George Wilson refused to talk to her at all. Then a few years later, when Shula got the head coaching job, he called me and said, 'Rosen, I'm not gonna let that girl with her miniskirt come around and interview our players.' I said, 'Don, that's what all the women are wearing these days.' Shula blew up. 'If she wears that thing again,' he said. 'I'll throw her out of the locker room myself.'

Rosen continued.

Joe DiMaggio was a spring training coach for the Yankees. He refused to be interviewed by a woman. But then Jane wisely said, 'Mr. Dimaggio, how would you feel if I lost my job because I didn't get an interview with the great Dimaggio?' Joe gave her the interview and told her, 'You know something dear, you really know your stuff.'

Bernie Rosen was a hands-on sports director for WTVJ for parts of an incredible sixty years. At this writing he is 94 years old and still sharp and wise.

"Local TV sports is being phased out in many markets, and to me it is a disgrace. They can claim ESPN has the highlights, but they only cover national stories. It's the local stations' responsibility to the community to cover local teams, thoroughly and insightfully."

A few years ago WTVJ took its local sports report off the news hour and it practically broke Bernie Rosen's heart. When I heard about this I wrote a letter to station manager Larry Olivitch condemning the move. Here's what I wrote:

Larry, I don't expect you to reconsider this decision or even return this email. I just want you to know that local sports and a community investment in it are as large as virtually any local news story, even those involving politics, crime, and city hall. A community like Miami has multiple pro and college sports teams and literally a hundred high school programs with stories and compelling interest from the public. I believe to withdraw cover-

age is an abandonment of the responsibility a local station has to its community.

Clearly your station doesn't think it matters. It does, Larry, maybe more than your executives realize. The Dolphins, Marlins, and Heat as well as the University of Miami have all won multiple championships and helped put South Florida on the map. Your map will not include coverage of these iconic symbols to the community. I find it sad and a dereliction of duty.

I never got a response. But Bernie Rosen saw the letter and his response was important to me.

"I want you to know how proud I am of you for writing what was on my mind. I spent 60 years believing in local sports coverage, and to see it taken away was deeply sad to me."

I will never forget that response from Bernie. I felt he taught me well—along with about a hundred other men and women. Everything I've accomplished in my career, and everything I've represented in broadcasting came from Bernie Rosen's teachings, and work ethic.

They may take a 4-minute sportscast off the local news, and it's deeply wrong. But they can never take away the lessons I learned, the fun I had, and the friends I made at WTVJ under the tutelage of Bernie Rosen.

And as silly as it sounds, it all started on a massage table with two guys named Bernie.

Crystal Clear

The year was 1974. Billy Crystal was 26 years old. He was light years away from becoming a comic icon, actor, and host of the Academy Awards. Back then he was a substitute teacher by day and stand-up comedian trying to find his voice at night. Little did he know that his life was about to change with a single phone call.

Muhammad Ali had just stunned the sports world by knocking out George Foreman in 8 rounds in Zaire, and sportscaster Dick Schaap was honoring Ali as *Sport* magazine's "Athlete of the Year" with a gala dinner at the Plaza Hotel in New York.

Schapp was trying to find a comedian who could perform a short routine about Ali for the dinner that would be televised locally on WCBS. Robert Klein was Schapp's first choice, but Klein was out of town. Klein's agent told Schaap that he had another young comic who'd just signed with the agency and who could do impressions of Ali and Howard Cosell. Schapp decided to book him. When Billy Crystal got the call he was excited to hear that he would be asked to perform the bit with Ali in attendance.

"I was feeding my daughter Jenny, who was 18 months old, when Schaap calls me out of the blue," says Crystal. "I didn't hesitate. This would be one of the biggest thrills and honors of my life. We walked into the Plaza Ballroom and my wife Janice and I looked like two people who were just coming to America… we were in awe."

Crystal added:

All kinds of people from all kinds of sports were there. Franco Harris was there. Archie Griffin was there. He had just won the Heisman. There was Gino Marchetti, Pete Rose, all of these gigantic stars … and then from a distance I saw Ali.

I was a gigantic fan. It wasn't just the boxing. It was all he meant to us. With the Kennedys gone and Martin Luther King gone, he was our voice. He was the one who told us to stand up for ourselves. And look what he sacrificed. What athlete today, still, would put it on the line for what he believed in like Ali did?"

Crystal was a virtual unknown at the time, but he was up on the dais just two seats to the right of his hero.

I'm thinking, Oh, my God. I'm walking in, like slow motion, like I'm in a Scorsese movie, and I'm in this amazing Steadicam shot, and he looks over at me, and I'm sure he's thinking, 'What is Joel Gray doing here? Who is this guy?' Schapp asks me how he should introduce me, and I say, jokingly, just introduce me as one of Ali's closest and dearest friends. Neil Simon was there. George Plimpton spoke. Everyone was great, and then they introduced me."

Crystal does the routine, and he's getting big laughs, including from the champ. Just then Ali's corner man and friend, Drew 'Bundini' Brown. begins to heckle Billy in a light-hearted way. Billy takes the heckle and runs with it.

It's the first TV show I ever appeared on and I'm getting heckled two minutes into my bit. I ad libbed 'I'll handle this, Bundini' as Howard Cosell. Ali was putting his napkin over his face. He was laughing hard now, pounding the table, and when I finished Ali picked me up and said, 'You're my little brother.' And that started the relationship.

Billy Crystal didn't know it then, but a close personal friendship was born that night, one that would last for nearly 43 years.

We did many events together, all kinds of events. He did stuff for me too. He was a host for an event for Hebrew University when I got the Scopus Award. He came and sat with us. Can you imagine a Black Muslim with a yarmulke on calling my mother 'mama'? And my mother sliced the challah in front of everyone and Ali said, 'Mama, I get to eat your magic bread.'

The "magic" between Ali and Crystal led to more appearances for both. In 1979, I saw Billy at the Forum in Los Angeles at Ali's retirement show. He did a brilliant, funny and touching piece about Ali's life from the beginning of his career to his dramatic win over Leon Spinks to win the title for the then-unprecedented third time. He wrote it expressly for the event. It was called "Fifteen Rounds."

In the Forum appearance, the director put Ali in an iso shot, so they show a picture of Ali watching me be him. It was surreal. Afterward I was just so lost in what had happened because it was very emotional. Ali comes up to me. I was standing with Richard Pryor, and he pushes Richard slightly aside and hugs me and says, 'Little brother, you made my life better than it was.'

Muhammad and Billy talked frequently and affectionately for years. When Billy toured his one-man show "700 Sundays" there was a stop in Phoenix near where Ali lived. The champ, his body now ravaged by Parkinson's, wanted to attend. Billy said:

He wasn't in great health. They got him ready for the show and I told his wife Lonnie that if he's in the audience, it could be a distraction. So we got him a reclining chair to watch from the wings. Just before intermission I tell the audience, 'Today is a special day. Muhammad Ali turned 65. I want you all to wish him a happy birthday.' And people started to applaud. Then I said, 'Wait...hold your applause...let me bring him out so you can say it to him....' We had a cake, and he loved it, and then did a little motion like I was crazy."

As Ali's health worsened it was harder and harder for the men to connect.

The last time I saw him was at a fundraiser for Parkinson's research, a great event called "Fight Night," also in Phoenix. Ali was too sick to even appear on stage. He could barely keep his head up and he was trembling terribly. They told me he wanted

to see me. When I got backstage, Ali's head was down. He was wearing dark sunglasses and I grabbed his hand. He squeezed it hard. He couldn't speak to me, but I knew Ali was 'in there.'"

Added Crystal:

"Ali never believed he was a victim of Parkinson's. Because as hard and painful as it was, he felt he was serving as an inspiration to others who suffered from this terrible disease."

Crystal would see perhaps his closest friend in show business also endure a neurological disease. In 2013 Robin Williams was diagnosed with Lewy Body dementia, a rare disease similar to Alzheimer's that, like Ali's Parkinson's, renders a person incapable of controlling muscle function, memory, and can cause hallucinations and depression. It was first in fact diagnosed as Parkinson's itself.

When Robin was diagnosed he called me from the doctor's office. I had never heard fear in his voice before. He told me, and I tried to play it down by saying I'd put him in touch with Ali's doctors, because they did great things with Parkinson's. And Robin would ask me from time to time... 'How long was Ali like this? What was the progression?'

Robin Williams stunned the world when he committed suicide in 2014. Billy was asked to perform a tribute to his dear friend on the Emmy Awards telecast that year.

"I was trying to put it into words. While I was stunned at losing my friend I was also trying to make sense of all of it. It was the hardest thing I ever had to do in my life.

I was sad and confused. It felt like losing a brother and I didn't see it coming. So I had THAT weight."

Less than twenty months later, Lonnie Ali called Billy and told him that Muhammad wasn't expected to survive the night. She wanted Billy to perform a tribute to his friend.

"The memorial for Ali was actually planned for some five years. When Lonnie told me he was dying I had less than ten days to summon up my thoughts, both humorous and inspiring, for some 17,000 people in Ali's hometown of Louisville, Kentucky."

But it was also a tribute for tens of millions watching all over the world. Crystal continued.

Bill Clinton was there. Bryant Gumbel, and a couple other people, and me. I had ten days to accept his death and then prepare for one of the most important moments in my life, and for hundreds of millions of people a very important moment for them too. It was an honor, an awesome responsibility and both my deep privilege and challenge to sum it all up. I was up all night the night before in Louisville and it was very emotional. It really hit me the day of the funeral, when thousands of people were running in the street after the funeral procession. It reminded me of Robert Kennedy's train and his funeral. It's a very hard task. Not just to summon up words for a global figure, but in remembering my own friendship and emotions for 40 years. It's global and personal at the same time. I wasn't just there as a celebrity. I was there as a friend.

Billy's tribute lasted about fourteen minutes. It was funny and sentimental, moving and deeply inspiring. Toward the end he said this of his friend, the champ.

He was a tremendous bolt of lightning created by mother nature out of thin air. A combination of power and beauty. We've all seen still photographs of lightning at the moment of impact. And in the moment of impact—ferocious in its strength, magnificent in its elegance—it lights up everything around it so you can see everything clearly.

Muhammad Ali struck us in the middle of America's darkest night, in the heart of America's most threatening gathering storm. His power toppled the mightiest of foes, and his intense light shed on America so that WE could see more clearly—in justice, in equality, poverty, pride, self-realization, courage, laughter, love, joy, religious freedom for all. Ali forced us to take a look at ourselves. This brash young man thrilled us, angered us, confused, challenged us, and he ultimately became a silent messenger of peace.

As Billy Crystal wrapped up his eulogy and remembrance, he referenced the great artists in human history, and he included Ali in that category.

Only once in a thousand years or so do we get to hear a Mozart, or see a Picasso, or read a Shakespeare. Ali was one of them. And yet, at his heart, he was still a kid from Louisville who ran with the gods and walked with the crippled, and laughed at the foolishness of it all ... But he will never die. He was my big brother.

Klein Time

Somewhere in the 70s when I was in college in Miami, long before I ever became a broadcaster, I had some strange illusion that maybe I would try my hand at stand-up comedy. I tried and mostly failed, cobbling together some sort of set at the locally-famous coffee house in Coral Gables called "The Flick."

I had no material. I actually "opened" (if you want to call it that) for people like Odetta, the folk legend, Dion of Dion and the Belmonts, and Etta James (later in her career). I had no real observations, just some corny old-school impressions, and I had no business anywhere near a stage or a microphone.

I decided to apply for the MC job at another club called "Bubba's," a brand new and short-lived cabaret room for the real pros. I got the job, and was thrilled to introduce some real comedy legends.

One night I introed a bizarre guy I had never heard of. He was brilliant and tore me apart with laughs because he parodied the entertainment business. Meet the 28 year-old Steve Martin. Turns out

that week at the club was one of his first extended engagements on the East Coast.

The manager told me that other big comedians were booked. Freddie Prinze was one of them, maybe George Carlin... and then he mentioned my comedy hero, Robert Klein.

Now I was riveted. "You mean Robert Klein is coming here?" I asked.

"For two shows; one night only," he replied.

Jerry Seinfeld, probably the greatest stand-up comedian of his generation, called Robert Klein "The Beatles" to him. Jay Leno had no furniture in his tiny apartment outside Boston as a kid. He did have a Robert Klein poster on his wall though. I had that poster too: Klein's "Child of the '50s" album.

Robert Klein was so much more than a comedy icon. He was literate, wise, outspoken, quick-witted, and thoughtful, but he could also be goofy and musical. And he knew what to do with a microphone. Klein was always confident and whimsical. He was and is the greatest observational comedian in my lifetime. I wanted to be like him. I just didn't have the material, talent, or confidence, or anything that made Klein great. He influenced a thousand stand-up comics... and a wannabe like me.

It was a Friday night in Coconut Grove and Klein was headlining. I think I did about three minutes of the worst material in comedy history. And then I got to say these words:

"Ladies and Gentlemen, Bubba's is proud to present...Robert Klein!"

The guy got a standing ovation before he hit the mic stand.

Klein told me recently that he began with only about seven minutes of material, and that he kicked off his career two months before JFK was shot—in September of 1963. It would be at least four or five years before he got any national attention. At the time he was a student at Alfred University (later her studied drama at Yale), living with his parents and trying to earn a buck as a substitute teacher. At first he had no real comedic ambition. He only worked stand-up because he didn't want to sit idle as an actor, waiting for roles that wouldn't come in, or enduring the rejection that's a fundamental part of the acting business. But then he started doing routines in

New York City's Greenwich Village.

With close friend Fred Willard he joined the Chicago improv group Second City. His first acting gig was a potato chip commercial for Ruffles. One of his first real comedy club dates was at Cafe Wha, which still stands on MacDougal Street in Manhattan. It was there where he got a strong positive reaction to his brand of humor. Then after working up the nerve he asked to audition at the Bitter End, an even more noteworthy club. Then it was on to The Improv, Catch a Rising Star and other top venues.

He had a good run and some positive responses. And then he hit a wall. Three weeks of nothing. Doubt began to set in. One night Rodney Dangerfield, who himself battled failure and self-doubt—quitting and then making comedy comebacks—saw Klein perform.

"I'll tell ya kid, that's fuckin' good stuff you have up there," said Dangerfield. "If you're willing to work every night for the next three years you can be great."

Dangerfield would eventually befriend Klein, and for years they were as close as Dangerfield could be with anyone, despite Rodney's distrusting and occasionally sour temperament.

"I never got to see Lenny Bruce perform live," Klein told me. "I always admired Lenny, and people like Mort Saul and Alan King, and later of course Richard Pryor, Jonathan Winters, and George Carlin. But Rodney was voice of encouragement and a critic who helped shape what I was doing and where I was going."

And Klein was going places indeed. He performed on dozens of talk shows, was a regular guest on *The Tonight Show*, *The Steve Allen Show* and others. He hosted a summer replacement program for the Smothers Brothers called *Comedy Tonight*, where he was told by CBS executives in no uncertain terms NOT to get political or face cancellation as the Brothers had.

He was one of the first hosts of *Saturday Night Live*. He recorded multiple comedy albums and performed on the massive Broadway hit "They're Playing our Song," written by Neil Simon. It was nominated for a Tony in 1979. 40 years later Klein and Lucie Arnaz are reviving their original roles for a one-night benefit on Broadway.

But back to Klein's multifaceted career:

He performed the first HBO special for stand-up comedians in

1975, following it with seven others. I spoke with him about artistic courage and devotion to a craft.

I started out as funny kid, and my father, who was in the textile business, was funny too, so there was no inhibition early on. I realize now that it takes some degree of courage, not like running into a fiery building mind you, but an artistic courage to get up in front of an audience as an unknown with a desire to make strangers laugh. But at the other end there's the successful comedian who has to constantly update and provide hours of new material, and to sell tickets and fill theaters.

I've never had a writer for my stand-up. I work only with a musical arranger and show organizer I bounce ideas off. It remains challenging and demanding, and I still love it. But up there, on stage, it's all me. Anyone who ever blames a bad show on a bad audience is full of crap. Your job is to be funny. If you're not, it's your fault.

Robert Klein has had one of the most storied careers in comedy history. He has acted in some 40 feature films and starred in both comedy and dramatic series, including, as I write this, NBC's *Will and Grace*. At the age of 76 he still performs dozens of stand-up shows for private and public audiences.

I perform in clubs where people really want to see me, and showrooms where wives drag their husbands to see me, to gated community centers where audiences go to bed at 8 o'clock in the evening. What is constant is the work and the desire to perform with my voice, my timing, my style, and my material. I still prepare shows geared to specific audiences. If I perform a show in Boise it doesn't mean anything to talk about DeWitt Clinton High School in the Bronx. But the demand is there and so is the audience. My job is to succeed by any means necessary.

Klein has always gravitated to political satire as far back as the Nixon era, and still does political material. But he has pulled back—not because of fear but because members of his audience no longer think the current administration is funny.

I understand people like Jerry Seinfeld and Jay Leno not performing political material. That's not their style and never was. But for me, if people are uncomfortable with a subject, I don't

push it much either. I pick my spots. I'll make fun of both Repub-
licans and Democrats. I have a bit where I say, for example, that
'Bill Clinton is a Rhodes scholar.....from the waist up. From the
waist down he's a high school sophomore trying to cop a feel from
a girl in biology class.'

But hypocrisy is still ripe material for Klein, especially the
"family values" crowd.

At least Eliot Spitzer didn't play the family values card. $3,500
for sex in this economy? I could have gotten him 12 girls with a
free towel. Larry Craig wanted to have sex in an airport men's
room, the one place I want to get out of as quickly as possible. En-
sign in Nevada... for schtupping his campaign manager's wife,
and got her a job at Quiznos, I think, shredding lettuce."

One night as he was leaving a Los Angeles restaurant, Klein was
video ambushed by TMZ cameras.

I know what they were doing, trying to get a rise out of me,
but it doesn't faze me. I fight back when they push me. I realize
that it's what they want. I was goaded, but I have never pulled
up my views of life, of the government, and never stop in my act
or even in a private setting where those creeps were looking for a
little red meat. Screw 'em. I'm not embarrassed or ashamed. They
should be.

Klein sees stand-up comedy differently these days.

With the internet and digital media and memes or whatever
the hell they call them, comedy is stolen or paraphrased and you
might even see some comics on cruise ships or small clubs directly
stealing material of mine and others from Youtube or from some
talk show. It's always been the case of ripoffs in comedy, but it's
more blatant now, and harder to stop. It's just the influence of
the web.

Robert Klein has performed his comedy material for more than
55 years. He's had one of the most diverse and decorated careers in
comedy history and has almost no regrets.

If it ended for me tomorrow I know I had the most fun, the
greatest career anyone could ask for, and I still get to do it, and
love it. I'm no angry or bitter comedian. I have a life and my fam-
ily and friends understand that I've always been me. I'm a person

who never took my persona too seriously. But my material has always been important to me. I'll never mail it in.

Talking to Klein on the phone, I was struck by his deep affection for his son, Allie, who at one point aspired to follow in his father's footsteps. Alexander Klein is now 34 years old and has decided to focus more on acting than stand-up.

I'm immensely proud of him. He decided to become an actor and he's a good one. I still see him on average 3 days a week and we are as close as a father and son could be.

Klein's first and only wife Brenda was an acclaimed opera singer, but Klein never remarried.

The divorce was very painful, but I made up my mind to make sure my son and I remained close. So even with my time on the road...whatever it took...private planes, turning down some work...my relationship with my son was the most important aspect of my life. I've worked virtually non-stop for more than 50 years and still the work is exciting and rich and really really fun. And it helps to know your son is well adjusted and happy.

Flash back to that time in the 70s at Bubba's. The job didn't last long and I was entering my senior year at the University of Miami. One night Robert Klein was booked for an on campus show. There were thousands of kids there. The air was heavy with excitement (and weed). Student entertainment director Kay Witten knew me as a minor radio personality on the college station and a baseball play-by-play man. She tapped me on the shoulder.

"Hey Roy, Robert Klein's opening act missed her flight. Can you fill in about a half hour until Klein shows up?"

I'm being asked to OPEN for Robert Klein!! Once again, I have no strong material. But unlike the earlier time I have something to fill the time. Like Klein (but not in his galaxy of ability or material), I find a premise—a bit about sports and athletes. And I'm getting a pulse from the audience. And then, incredibly, some laughs. I'm up there for 20 minutes and it's going pretty well. I have no illusions but I'm filling time for my comedy hero...Robert Klein!

Finally he arrives. He thanks me in front of the audience for "pulling it off." They gave me $100 bucks for my trouble. It was my first paid stand-up gig...and it was opening for Robert Klein. It was like taking batting practice with the Yankees!

45 years later I tell Klein the story. Of course he doesn't remember it, but then he says:

"Roy, you're an interviewer and a broadcaster." And then with a laugh he recalls Rodney Dangerfield's advice: "If you're willing to work every night for three years, you might get good at it." I laugh too.

Somehow I'd rather watch a pro do it then try it myself. Yet, true enough, these days I perform a one-man show about sports. It's got some funny clips, a few jokes and music, and though I make a good living at it, I know I'll never be anything close to someone like Robert Klein.

But for a few minutes, when I was 20 years old, I shared a stage with my comedy hero. For all the many thrills and accomplishments in my life, I get to say that! It was Robert Klein that got me to the microphone. Years later he came on my show and I finally got to thank him. Life is sure interesting, isn't it?

Coming Home

I was lucky.

I was hired as a TV sports anchor in my hometown of Miami, Florida when I was, incredibly, just 21 years old!

It was a dream come true.

I became a minor celebrity. Girls who'd never gave me a moment's notice suddenly were interested in me. I got to meet all the top athletes of the day and interview them, and the phone rang with PR firms offering ideas for stories because they said, "I was their favorite sportscaster," even though I knew it was just a come-on. Still, I had the greatest job in the world. After 80 bucks a week as an intern, I was making the astronomical sum of $250 a week. Then one Friday in 1976 I was called into the office: and I was fired.

I felt like Cinderella at midnight. My heart was crushed. My father was shocked and heartbroken, and now the phone stopped ringing and people started talking in whispers behind my back.

That was 43 years ago. I thought I'd never work again… certainly not with a job that meant so much, in a place I loved, and at a TV station where so many of my friends and colleagues were so friendly and affectionate to me.

I was the kid. I was "Roy boy" or "Roysie," the young pup who lit up the newsroom with laughs and fun.

It was all over. Or so I thought.

Within six months I was hired by KNXT in Los Angeles, and I've been in LA ever since. Over the years I've gotten jobs in broadcasting that I could never have imagined in my wildest dreams.

I tell this story because 43 years later I went back to those old friends … to my "class" reunion at WPLG-TV in Miami.

For me reunions are always a mixed bag. As time passes faces and names grow more distant, and the memories more vague and foggy. As I walked into that restaurant there were some people I knew immediately, and the love, affection, and friendships were alive again. Some I didn't recognize, and some names were foreign to me. But that night I was something of a folk hero to more than a few.

I was, for the evening, the kid who got canned and who somehow picked himself up and made good: had a national TV show, and showed the people who'd cut me loose that I could, after all, prove management wrong and achieve something after that crushing dismissal.

At that party was the very news director who'd fired me 43 years earlier. I'd thought about what I'd say, and honestly, I'd briefly considered that if I were to meet this person (whom I will not identify) I would be smug or sarcastic .

But that's not really me. Instead I decided to be grateful. I walked up and simply said, "Thank you. Thank you for firing me. I was green and I needed someone, somehow, to kick me in the pants, metaphorically, and force me to knock on new doors, and even kick them in."

I found that graciousness and humility and even a weird kind of appreciation worked best. Some people knew the meeting might happen, and that it might be a tense moment for both of us. Instead it was a moment of satisfaction, good will and cordiality.

Almost everyone in that room had retired from broadcasting. I'm lucky that I am still active in my career and I don't ever want to stop doing what I love. Some dear friends have passed, and others have simply quit the business and gone on to other things.

But after all these years, I have come to believe that humility, grace, and magnanimity are all part of becoming a mature human being.

At least I hope so.

And so that night I drank a toast to yesterday, and with it a bow to all the blessings and goodwill people have given me in my life.

Thomas Wolfe wrote that you can't go home again. But at my Channel 10 reunion, going home, albeit briefly, was sweet, joyous, and welcoming.

Thanks, WPLG in Miami, for all you gave me. I'm a very, very blessed man. And I'll always be grateful.

It was nice to be home.

Full Circle

I had some houseguests not long ago. Dear friends stayed with me and I wanted to give them my undivided attention. It was a lot more than having a few old college buddies over. It was a very, very, special reunion and one I will never forget as long as I live.

I began this book with the experiences as a batboy for the Baltimore Orioles. During that time I made some very close friends.

This weekend two of them stayed with me. And for 72 hours, time stood still.

Brooks Robinson and Jim Palmer were my houseguests for the weekend.

They came to town for Frank Robinson's celebration of life ceremony at Dodger Stadium.

Brooks' eldest son Brooks David also joined us. It was a kind of adult slumber party with two of baseball's greatest players, Hall of Famers both.

I wouldn't dream of letting them stay at a hotel, and wouldn't think of allowing them to rent a car or use any kind of service. So I picked them up at the airport, and for the weekend, any wish from them was not just my command. It was my extreme pleasure.

My honor.

Jim Palmer and I have been friends for close to 50 years. We maintain a very playful and funny relationship, and I cherish it.

But Brooks is something, someone else. To me he's royalty, only he's never thought of himself that way.

He's had some health issues, and his gait is slower, but his mind and spirit are still sharp.

When Brooks and his son came to my house—a place decorated

in Orioles memorabilia—I didn't want to embarrass him by making it look like it was a shrine to him. But I also have to be who I am. I didn't take many things down.

Instead of feeling embarrassed, Brooks looked at my collection with wonder and joy. He loved my Beatles room and my collection of rock and roll memorabilia and jukeboxes. To watch them sit and enjoy my train set (Brooks has one too) was a thrill too. But the guys were mostly content to reminisce and trade stories.

Brooks Robinson was perhaps the most beloved person I have ever known in my life, and not because he worked at it, *but precisely because he didn't.*

He didn't "dish," nor did he do "snark," and he would never ever have told stories out of school. That most of all may be why people loved him so much. As great a player as he was, with 16 Gold Gloves, he never ever pulled any kind of rank, never felt entitled to anything. Class isn't something you work at. You either have it or you don't, and your manner dictates it. Classy people never talk about themselves and never use their names in the third person.

In all the years I've known Brooks Robinson, it never occurred to him that he was BROOKS ROBINSON.

Palmer is funny, acerbic and a storyteller. We laughed for hours recounting war stories and inside jokes. Brooks let Palmer do the "entertaining".

I could say so many things about that weekend, but some are matters of the heart—mine—so I'll keep most to myself. But I will share one intimacy.

At dinner it was time to toast my friends. Toasting Palmer was easy and funny, but then I turned to Brooks and said this:

"I want you to know—and you do—how much I love you and cherish you. And you must know you are my hero and always will be."

Then I started to cry.

Brooks looked at me and said, "I love you too Roy, and always will."

Then Brooks David said something that made me feel like a million bucks.

"Roy, I love you because you love my dad."

The weekend was so joyous and warm and wonderful, and Palmer kept it funny and alive with hysterical banter. And the love was everywhere.

We all attended Frank's memorial on Sunday, and Brooks was asked to speak about his late comrade. "Frank was about winning," he said. "And when we won with him, we won something more than baseball games ... we won as people. Just knowing him was a win. I'm a better man from having known him."

Then we went back to my place.

Brooks slept in my bedroom, because the King gets the best room and the best bed.

I slept in the guest room. I wouldn't have had it any other way.

When the weekend was over I dropped Brooks and Brooks David off at the airport. Palmer drove back to his home.

When I got back I was alone in my house. I took a deep breath. My childhood heroes had been my houseguests for the weekend, and I cherished every moment, every second. I'll never forget it.

I was introduced to becoming a sportscaster directly because of Brooks. He was my first interview when I was just 14. But far more than that, he was an inspiration.

He is a man of character and generosity and grace, and he specializes in human decency. I have never met a more decent and beloved person in all my life.

How I carry myself in life came from my parents, and from Brooks.

I only hope I've served them well.

The house was quiet and the week ahead was to be a busy one for me. But for that weekend it had been alive with memories, laughter, and a ton of love.

As I dropped the Robinsons off at the curb we hugged tightly, and I watched Brooks walk into the terminal. My eyes got misty again as he disappeared.

You never know about life. You never know how much time you have left with people you dearly love. Nothing is guaranteed for anyone.

So I was so deeply satisfied and grateful that our time the past weekend was so very well spent, and the words were spoken out loud, not kept away or protected.

My God, how wonderful a life I've had. So many joys, so many experiences.

This weekend ranked right near the top.

To borrow Brooks' line about Frank, "I'm a better man for having known them."

Made in the USA
Middletown, DE
18 September 2019